QUILTED
PLANET

A SOURCEBOOK OF QUILTS FROM AROUND THE WORLD

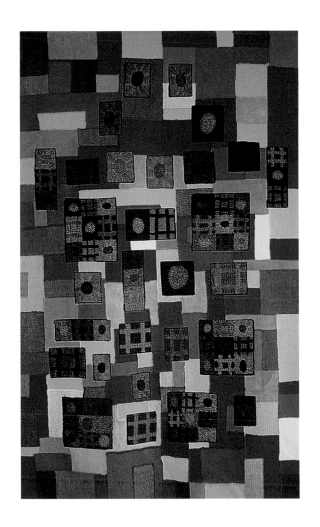

CELIA EDDY

QUILTED PLANET

A SOURCEBOOK OF QUILTS FROM AROUND THE WORLD

MITCHELL BEAZLEY

Quilted Planet
Celia Eddy
For my daughter, Vaseema Hamilton, my grand-daughter Alice Maud
Hamilton, and to the memory of my father, Lewis Grenfell Huddy.

First published in Great Britain in 2005 by Mitchell Beazley,
an imprint of Octopus Publishing Group Ltd,
2–4 Heron Quays, London E14 4JP

ISBN 1 84533 009 9

A CIP record for this book is available from the British Library

Senior Executive Editor   Anna Sanderson
Executive Art Editor   Auberon Hedgecoe
Design   Vivienne Brar
Senior Editor   Emily Anderson
Editor   Catherine Blake
Picture Research   Emma O'Neill
Production   Seyhan Esen

Set in Bliss and The Sans
Colour origination by Bright Arts, HK
Printed and bound in China by Toppan Printing Company Ltd

ABOVE "Cosmos" by Dianne Firth, 2003,
Australia. This quilt was inspired by the stars
in the night sky. The artist is a landscape
architect by profession but says, "when I
need to recharge my soul I turn to the
heavens". Techniques used include
discharge dyeing and machine-quilting.

PAGE 1 "Sind Fragments" by Frieda
Oxenham, Scotland. The original inspiration
for this quilt was a jacket from Sind, India –
echoed in the hand-dyed colours of the
cottons. Black appliqué pieces are covered
in running stitch using contrasting colours.

PAGE 2 "In the Pink" by Sandie Lush, 2002,
England. This contemporary interpretation
of the classic North Country strippy quilt
displays superb hand-quilting (the hallmark
of this artist's work), whereby she pays
homage to the skill and craftsmanship
of the fine quilters of yesteryear.

CONTENTS

INTRODUCTION

"The history of the world can be read in textiles." John Gillow and Bryan Sentance, *World Textiles*

It must first be made clear that the word "quilt" is used in this book in the broadest possible sense, in order to include all the various techniques associated with quiltmaking. The best-known technique today, at least in Western cultures, is patchwork, but many others, such as appliqué and embroidery, also feature.

Quilting exists almost everywhere on the planet, but each region has its own quilting styles and techniques that have evolved from very varied histories and cultural traditions. Some are specific to a particular time and place, such as the 19th-century Baltimore album quilts of the USA. Others, such as crazy patchwork, which has its origins in various cultures but reached its zenith in Victorian England, have been influential in many different countries over a long period of time.

All these traditional styles and techniques have deep roots. Surprisingly often, their gradual evolution can be traced back hundreds, or even thousands, of years, and all bear witness to the universal and perennial love of needlecraft that unites all quiltmakers. That immense diversity and richness could scarcely be dealt with in any one book, however large. So *Quilted Planet* aims to provide a series of "snapshots" of the styles and techniques that have flourished over many centuries, and in many different regions of the world. It is hoped that these will inspire quiltmakers everywhere both to look more closely at their own traditions and to consider and learn from those of other cultures and communities.

Much of the work of today's quilt artists may seem far removed from any particular tradition, but even the most innovative quilt art has, to some extent, evolved from what were once local cultures and practices. Indeed, many

LEFT Mid-18th-century "hunger cloth" from the Catholic parsonage at Geldern, Lower Rhine, Germany. According to some sources, there evolved during the 11th century a custom of hanging a textile, known as a "hunger cloth", in front of the altar, starting on the fifth Sunday of Lent. Interpretations of the religious symbolism of this practice vary – one equates it with Jesus veiling his divinity during his passion. This is a superb example of European ceremonial patchwork, in which many small pieces of cloth have been painstakingly joined together from behind, edge-to-edge, to depict the story of Christ's sufferings.

RIGHT Indo-Portuguese silk quilt, early 17th century, in which the Eastern influence on early European silk quilts can clearly be seen. Once Portuguese colonists had opened trading posts in India, cotton, linen, and silk quilts were commissioned from Indian needle-workers. Silk quilts were the height of luxury and only affordable by the very wealthy. Here, yellow silk is richly embroidered with silk thread in many colours. In the centre are two birds facing each other under a crown – a Portuguese symbol – while Hindu mythological figures appear in the corners.

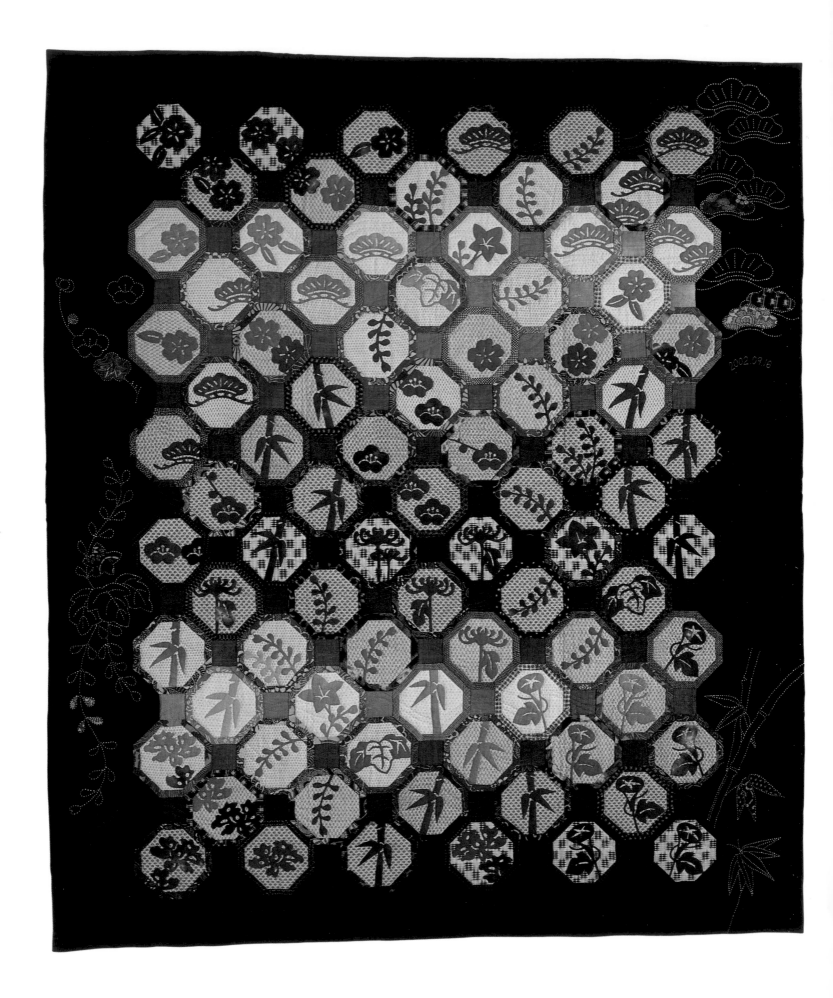

contemporary cutting-edge quilt artists acknowledge the importance and value of this quilting heritage, and consciously seek to reinterpret old styles in a modern way. The difference between the world of the past and the "global village" of today is that now, potentially, we all have access to not just one tradition but also to the whole, immeasurably rich variety of quilting across time and space. Many quilt artists have already realized this, and have referred to this diversity in their work. Some of these contemporary reinterpretations are included in this book's journey around the wide world of quilting, because they show more vividly than any words can do just how much vitality these traditions still possess, and how inspirational they remain.

The basic idea of stitching through layers of fabric goes back thousands of years. What is more, right from the beginning quilts were made with the intention of producing textiles that would be both practical and aesthetically pleasing. In the first place, stitching the layers together was intended just to anchor them, to make them warmer, more solid, and longer lasting, but almost always, even from the very earliest times, there was also an intention to create something attractive.

What is thought to be the oldest surviving example of quilting, for instance, was discovered near the border between Mongolia and Siberia, on the floor of a Scythian chieftain's tomb. It is thought to date from between 100BC and AD200, but many of the decorative patterns on this quilt, such as spirals and cross-hatching, are still used by today's wholecloth quilters. Clearly, the makers of this quilt felt that, in death as much as in life, a chieftain should be surrounded by furnishings that reflected his high status. Another ancient example of quilting comes in what may seem to us today an unusual form. It is a shoe, made out of quilted felt, patched with leather. Found on one of the great highroads of the ancient world, the Silk Road, it probably dates from between AD750 and 860. The pattern on this example is still used by quilters

LEFT *The Martyrdom of St Ursula* by Hans Memling, 1498. In this side panel from the Shrine of St Ursula, now in the Memling Museum in Bruges, the soldier in the left foreground is wearing quilted armour. It is generally believed that the quilting technique was brought to Europe about 800 years ago by the Crusaders, who, fighting in their heavy forged iron, had been defeated by the Saracens wearing light quilted shirts and chain mail. The quilted armour, made of linen stuffed with padding, was no longer effective after the introduction of firearms.

today, who usually describe its series of arcs as "Baptist Fan Quilting" or "Rainbow Quilting".

QUILTED ARMOUR

Perhaps not many people these days are likely to want to make quilted shoes, but quilted clothing is one of the oldest forms of quilting. Quilted clothing was used as armour, over a long period and in many areas, because it was possible to make it tough enough to provide a significant level of protection against arrows and swords. (Of course, once guns of any power were introduced the custom of quilting military clothing faded away fairly rapidly!)

The practice was probably most deeply rooted in the Far East, and there are many examples from China, Korea, India, and Japan; the quilted campaign vest illustrated on page 18 is a good example. But a painted panel in a German church, made as late as the end of the 15th century, still shows a sword-carrying knight dressed in a striped and quilted coat. There is even a theory that it was the introduction into Europe of quilted clothing as armour, perhaps brought back by the Crusaders from their

OPPOSITE "Kajin" by Kazuyo Kudo, an imaginative fusion of old and new by a contemporary Japanese quilt artist. Octagons have been tessellated with squares – a familiar patchwork pattern. Each of the octagons has been carefully cut from part of a plain or printed indigo fabric to highlight a particular plant or flower. The embroidery in the borders reflects a distinctive, and unmistakably Japanese, sense of style.

BELOW Patchwork altar valance, probably 8th century. It is one of an important collection of antiquities discovered in the Caves of the Thousand Buddhas – sanded-in caves situated along the Silk Road, explored by archeologists early in the 20th century. Such valances were seen in most Buddhist temples and give an indication of the value placed on even the smallest scraps of silk. This valance was probably a votive offering, perhaps made by pilgrims; it contains triangular patches and flags of patched, multicoloured chevrons pieced from fragments of precious silks from the Tang dynasty – no doubt the most valuable gift that poor people could offer.

campaigns in the East, that led first to quilting on every-day clothing and then to decorative bed furnishings.

During the 14th century, references to quilts, and in particular to quilted bedding, begin to appear more frequently than in earlier times, and there are some well-known pieces that survive from that period. Three quilts of Sicilian origin, dating from around 1395, provide awe-inspiring evidence of the brilliant standard of workmanship that went into them, probably carried out in a workshop. Two of these quilts were made as a pair, one of which is now in the Victoria and Albert Museum in London, the other in the Bargello Museum in Florence. The quilts are worked in squares and rectangles, each containing scenes and inscriptions telling the story of the legendary hero Tristan. The London quilt is worked with back stitches through two layers of heavy linen, suggesting that it would have been used as a wall hanging rather than as a bed quilt.

PATCHWORK AND QUILTING

"Patchwork? Ah, no! It was memory, imagination, history, joy, sorrow, philosophy, religion, romance, realism, life, love, and death; and over all, like a halo, the love of the artist for his work and the soul's longing for earthly immortality."
Eliza Calvert Hall, *Aunt Jane of Kentucky*

In his book *The Spirit of Folk Art*, Henry Glassie asks us to think of the kanthas of Bangladesh as offering "gifts to the mind". Their meaning, he says, lies in their technology. In stitching together and embroidering the fragments

of cloth that go to make up a kantha, the quilter is reassembling both the cloth and the universe. In Japan, too, the preservation of old fabrics is not just a sensible piece of thrift – it is a spiritual exercise with a symbolic meaning. A gift of a patchwork garment made out of treasured scraps of old fabric, for instance, carries with it the donor's hope that the recipient will have a life as long as that of the cloth. In fact, belief in the talismanic function of patchwork is quite widespread, in both Asia and Africa. In Indonesia a special patchwork jacket called an *antakusuma* is credited with magical powers of protection, while chiefs of certain tribes in Ghana wore robes of patchwork and appliqué as a mark of their status.

Another remarkable discovery made alongside that famous ancient route, the Silk Road, exemplifies the way in which simple patchworking could produce items that were both beautiful and rich with religious meaning. In a cave on the border between Mongolia and China, archaeologists found a spectacular Buddhist altar valance (below), probably dating from between AD700 and 800 and lovingly pieced together out of tiny scraps of silk. Even in many parts of Europe, patchwork and quilting techniques were used not only for producing domestic items, such as bed coverings and clothes, but also in a religious context, for vestments or church decorations.

Throughout Asia, patchworked textiles (often combined with appliqué or embroidery, or both, and sometimes quilted as well) were, and in many places still are, used

for items that are as much for show as for use: blankets for horses or oxen and decorations for elephants, as well as domestic items such as bags, are made in exuberant patterns and colours. In the Kutch region of India patchwork quilts are an indispensable part of a bride's dowry; the materials for them are mainly scraps of worn-out clothes, which indicate by their colours the status and tribal membership of the wearer.

In Europe, quilting (as distinct from patchwork) eventually evolved into a highly skilled and decorative form of needlework. Such elaborate and expensive virtuosity can be seen in the many surviving capes, jackets, petticoats, and gowns made for affluent 18th-century women across the whole continent. However, the finest examples of such sophisticated work are probably the exquisite wholecloth quilts produced at that time in Provence. Eventually, particularly in Britain, a rich repertoire of regional styles and patterns developed.

There is evidence to suggest that, to an extent, ornamental as well as utilitarian quilting has a long history in other parts of Europe as well. Early records show that fine quilting was regarded as another branch of the embroiderer's skill. It was used mainly for household items and clothing made for royal or noble households who could afford to pay for such high-quality and labour-intensive work. Quilting was frequently used as a background to embroidery on bed hangings, valances, coverlets, and pillows. Such work would often have been undertaken by professional embroiderers in towns and cities, who would probably be members of an embroiderers' guild.

Patchwork and quilting were, of course, also carried out by poor people for poor people. Such work was quick and crude, and the results were coarse but practical. These items were not meant to be things of beauty, they were simply intended to keep their overworked and under-nourished makers warm. The result was that in some areas patchwork eventually became associated

with poverty. That stigma did much to devalue patch-working and quilting, and no doubt gave rise to the notion that the patchwork quilt began as bedding for the poor. However, the great diversity of fabrics, many of which would have been available only to the affluent, in some 17th- and 18th-century quilts is evidence that in Europe patchwork was not confined to one stratum of society. Indeed, the fine silk and satin patchworks made in Victorian Britain emerged from an affluent middle-class who had time for creative needlework and ready access to expensive fabrics.

ABOVE Embroidered and quilted cotton kantha from East Bengal, Bangladesh, c.1920. The central design features a lotus (the symbol of the manifestation of life), with leaf borders and bird motifs. The fact that there are no people in the design suggests that this textile may have been worked by a Muslim woman, because living beings are not usually represented in Islamic art.

AMERICAN QUILTS

"America is not like a blanket – one piece of unbroken cloth, the same color, the same texture, the same size. America is more like a quilt – many pieces, many colors, many sizes, all woven and held together by a common thread." The Reverend Jesse Jackson

In early 19th-century America the snobberies of a settled social system had yet to establish themselves, at least in the west. Pioneers, after all, were all pioneers together!

And America had the added advantage of a palette of varied styles brought by immigrants from across the whole of Europe. It was in America, therefore, that the practical necessity of making something to keep you warm at night was finally and consistently turned into a genuine folk art. Not a single art, of course, because, as Jesse Jackson suggested, there is not a single America but many, and richly varied, Americas. Each cultural group has its own "take" on patchwork and quilting, its own particular

LEFT The earliest known example of dated patchwork, discovered in England in 2000. It is worked mainly in 12cm (4½in) squares, with the date, 1718, and the initials "E.H." pieced into one of the squares. The fabrics are predominantly silk, although some pieces of wool velvet are also included. The coverlet is worked in the style known as English patchwork, where the patches are basted over paper then oversewn together, and prefigures the development of patchwork as a technique in itself (where the pattern is achieved solely by the combination of colours and shapes). In earlier works, of which the quilt shown on the front cover of the book is an outstanding example, the patchwork serves merely as a background for appliqué and embroidery.

RIGHT Silk patchwork coverlet made by Mary Jane Scott of Northumberland, England, during the latter part of the 19th century. A superb example of Victorian patchwork in the classic English "frame" style, it contains silk, velvet, and satin. Brilliant, jewel-like colours are emphasized by the use of contrasting black patches. The narrow borders framing each section of patchwork add definition and unity to the complex design. The quilt was documented by the Quilters' Guild of the British Isles during the early 1990s, and the variety and quality of its fabrics make it a rare exception to the vast majority of documented frame quilts, which were usually made of cotton.

choice of style and technique from the vast array available in that privileged country. The unparalleled diversity of possible styles, together with the unbroken continuity of patchworking and quilting that has persisted since the time of the earliest settlers, makes America a source of inspiration for quilters across the world.

In fact, within a single country, American patchworking and quilting exemplifies just the sort of cross-fertilization of traditions it is hoped this book will help to bring about, wherever it is read. In many countries this is already, and increasingly, happening. Contemporary Japanese quilts, for example, often show clear signs of having been influenced by American traditions, but they show equally clearly that their makers have reinterpreted those traditions in the light of their own culture. The results are both stunning and heart-warming – an example to us all!

QUILTS AS ART

In an age when patchwork and quilting are becoming ever more eclectic, when practitioners seek to expand their horizons and eagerly borrow and adapt styles and traditions from all over the world, and when the line between quilts and textile art is rapidly disappearing, we might do well to ponder the words of W.B. Yeats. Writing in 1901, he observed: "Folk art is, indeed, the oldest of the aristocracies of thought, and because it refuses what is passing and trivial, the merely clever and pretty, as certainly as the vulgar and insincere, and because it has

LEFT Pieced and appliquéd cotton Civil War memorial quilt, made by Mary Bell Shawvan, c.1863. This is a good example of the way in which the American patchwork quilt became a unique repository of social and personal history. According to family history, Mary made the quilt for her husband, John, while she awaited his return from the war. He never saw the quilt – he died from wounds received at the notoriously bloody two-day battle at Chickamauga in Tennessee. When the Civil War began thousands of women took up quilting, to provide both quilts for soldiers and gifts for them on their return.

RIGHT Classic example of a "Centre Medallion" quilt in the English style, made in Maryland c.1820. The centre star is surrounded by ten borders pieced from plain and printed fabrics. The influence of the English style on American patchwork extended into the early 19th century, after which the trend was to use blocks to build up the top quilt.

gathered into itself the simplest and most unforgettable thoughts of the generations, it is the soil where all great art is rooted."

The quilts and quilting traditions in this book are organized geographically. Each historical account is illustrated by examples and followed by a selection of pieces by contemporary quiltmakers of the region, some of whom will have been inspired by local culture and traditions, others will have been inspired by landscape, perhaps, or by an aspect of regional life. However, all the artists featured are quiltmakers who are bringing new life to an ancient folk art.

For each of the major quilting traditions, pages documenting methods and styles offer a brief insight into the practicalities involved in creating the various types of quilts. It is not intended as a "how to", but if you want to pursue a particular subject, there is a list of relevant books and resources at the end of this book to help you on your way.

The aim has been to cover as many geographical areas as possible, but no single book could do justice to the amazing diversity and sheer number of patchwork and quilting traditions that exist throughout the world. There are also quilt artists and traditions in many places that still need to be researched and written about. However, it is hoped that the rich diversity of quilt art presented here will be enough to amaze and inspire.

Happy reading – and happy quilting!
Celia Eddy

All the colour and exoticism associated

historically with Asia and the Far East are

reflected abundantly in the patchwork and

quilting traditions of those regions of the

world. Seen and used everywhere, whether as

bedding, clothing, or bags, for robes or wrapping

ASIA AND THE FAR EAST

cloths, as decorations for pack animals or

decorative hangings for festivals, they are a vast

repository of social history and customs. Ethnic

textiles and sophisticated artifacts speak of

the lives of people of many tribes and castes,

and tell the history of civilizations. Rich with

pattern and symbolism, these textiles are a

treasury of inspiration for today's quiltmakers.

JAPAN : HISTORY AND TRADITIONS

Few patchwork and quilting traditions are as fascinating and diverse as those of Japan. One of the earliest documented uses for quilted fabric is as bedding. Indeed, the word "quilt" is derived from the Latin *culcita*, meaning a mattress or pillow. Taking its origins from this is the futon – a stitched or tied quilt laid on the floor, on which traditionally the Japanese sleep, with another quilt on top for a cover. This is a very flexible arrangement as the covering quilt can be changed according to the season: thick, warm quilts for winter use and lighter quilts or simply sheets for the summer. In the past, the style and material of these quilts reflected the prosperity of the owner – the more affluent had elaborately decorated and embroidered silk quilts, while less wealthy people slept under indigo-dyed cotton quilts.

YOSEGIRE

Although rarely seen these days, heavy winter top quilts in the shape of a kimono were once very popular. In rural areas these would often be made from patchwork stitched from fabric scraps, very simply pieced in large squares and rectangles arranged symmetrically. This technique is known as *yosegire*, meaning "to collect" or "to gather", and originated in the desire to prolong the life of fabrics at a time when they were scarce and therefore valuable.

Yosegire can be compared to the style of patchwork known as "crazy" patchwork, which became popular in the West in the latter half of the 19th century (*see* pages 62–5). However before that, during the 1830s, a fashion developed in Japan for women to organize scraps in this style to make clothing and various household items, and to cover screens. It has been suggested that it was *yosegire*, used on screens displayed at an exhibition of Japanese decorative arts at the Philadelphia Centennial Exposition in 1876, that caught the Western imagination and sparked the craze for that style of patchwork. In Japan the pattern became such a vogue that it was stencil-dyed onto cloth and hand-made paper, examples of which can still be found today.

PREVIOUS PAGE "Dream Windows" by Shizuko Kuroha, 2001. The meeting of East and West is symbolized in this contemporary quilt; a synthesis of American-inspired "Log Cabin" pattern and quintessentially Japanese indigo fabrics creates a complex quilt surface, rich in pattern and colour.

BELOW In Japan, as in many other cultures, there is sound evidence for the early use of quilting in armour. This is well illustrated by this campaign vest, which dates from the late 16th century and is both functional and highly decorative. It belonged to Toyotomi Hideyoshi, a famous ruler who lived between 1537 and 1598, and was probably made from pre-quilted cotton brought from India by a British trader. Its existence suggests that armour was a recognized application of quilting in Japan at that time. The back of the vest is decorated with appliqué depicting a stylized pawlonia flower.

ABOVE *Kosode* is the traditional name for what is today considered an ordinary kimono. Unlike the classic court kimono, it has short, practical sleeves, which give it its name. *Kosode* began to be used as top-wear during Japan's medieval period, and quickly became fashionable during the Edo period (1600–1868). The pattern on this example, dating from around 1700, was developed from the patchwork technique known as *kirihame*, which can be traced back as clothing decoration to the year 1056.

PATCHWORK

Historically, Japanese patchwork has religious significance. In Shinto, the predominant religion, all things, animate and inanimate, are imbued with a spirit and this, of course, includes textiles. In ancient times fabric was so revered and highly valued that sometimes it was used as a form of currency, and fabrics were given as tribute to emperors and warlords. This reverence reflected not only their scarcity in pre-industrial Japan but also the Shinto philosophy. Even today old textiles have symbolic meaning, and the care and preservation of textiles is seen as a spiritual exercise: the giving of a patchwork garment, for example, conveys a wish for long life for the recipient.

BUDDHIST ROBES

It was an important precept in Japanese Buddhism that monks should renounce ostentation and wealth. *Kesa*, patched robes made from recycled fabrics, were an outward manifestation of their vows. The *kesa* is a flat rectangle, usually about 2–3m (6–9ft) long, worn across the body and passing under the right arm and over the left shoulder. The patchwork is built up in a series of panels of an uneven number, as decreed by the Buddha.

BELOW Seven-band *kesa*, 19th century, silk fabric with laminated silver and gold paper. The piecing is so fine and complicated that it is difficult to identify the seven bands. Affluent people believed that there was spiritual virtue in giving to monasteries and temples, and they would naturally donate the more expensive fabrics used in their own clothing. As a result, *kesa* became quite sumptuous and they also often displayed a marked degree of aesthetic awareness, as illustrated here.

RIGHT When a Japanese woman reaches the age of 20 she traditionally wears a special garment called a *furisode*, which is the formal kimono for single women and signals that she is available for marriage. It is usually made of brightly coloured, fine silk and is distinguished from ordinary kimonos by its very long sleeves. This example, dating from the late 19th century, is believed to have been worn by a Kyoto courtesan. It is pieced in the *yosegire* style in silk crêpe, featuring four colours and six types of pattern.

SASHIKO

The style of Japanese quilting called *sashiko*, which means "little stabs", is a unique combination of quilting and embroidery. *Sashiko* has practical origins: it was used to stitch together layers of textiles, which in early times were tough fabric woven from grasses and other plant fibres. It was made into strong, durable clothing to be worn for heavy work in the fields, and was used for this purpose up until the 1950s. Very few examples of old *sashiko* survive, because they were inevitably worn out and thrown away.

The decorative use of *sashiko* and the patterns that we see today developed largely in the 18th century, when there was increased prosperity in Japan and inexpensive cotton fabrics became more readily available. Many of the patterns seen in *sashiko* have been used for hundreds of years. Some of them have symbolic significance: for example, the hexagonal grid represents the shell of a tortoise and, by extension, implies a wish for long life and prosperity. Today quiltmakers from all over the world have adopted *sashiko* as a favourite technique. They enjoy experimenting with traditional styles and patterns, and incorporating them into their own quilt art.

LEFT This fireman's coat, dating from the early 20th century, is heavily quilted in plain running stitch and has a decorative lining. *Sashiko* was used to quilt layers of coats together, which would then be drenched with water before the firefighter got to work. During the parades that were held to honour the firefighters, the coat would be worn with the best side on display.

RIGHT Double-layered, indigo-dyed work coat, early to mid-20th century, showing two different *sashiko* patterns, one for the outer layer of the coat and another for the lining. Originally *sashiko* stitching was used as a way of repairing and strengthening fabric, and work garments such as this would have been stitched in a plain running stitch. Decorative *sashiko* was an 18th-century development, as by then cheap, warm clothing was more widely available, so women had leisure-time to create decorative items instead.

SASHIKO: METHOD AND STYLE

Sashiko is a form of hand-sewing using a simple running stitch to make repeating or interlocking patterns. It is usually seen on indigo-dyed cotton, but other materials such as silk or wool, and even colours and prints, are popular nowadays. Tightly woven evenweave fabrics are a good choice for patterns stitched in straight lines, because you can count the threads to get even stitches. The usual stitch count is five to eight stitches per inch, and it is important that the stitches are as even and regular in length as possible. *Sashiko* may be worked through one or more layers of fabric, with or without wadding. Traditional *sashiko* thread is 100 per cent cotton and is heavier than normal quilting thread, but other good choices include crochet thread, cotton perle, and embroidery silks. Any embroidery or ordinary sewing needle suitable for the thread can be used.

LEFT Most *sashiko* patterns have specific names and are stylized representations of the natural world, such as clouds, plants, birds, and so on. The pattern at the top is called "*Yama Sashi*", or "Mountain Pattern", while below is a version of "*Kaki no Hana*", or "Persimmon Flower". Some of the oldest *sashiko* designs were originally stitched by counting warp and weft threads on coarse hemp fabric.

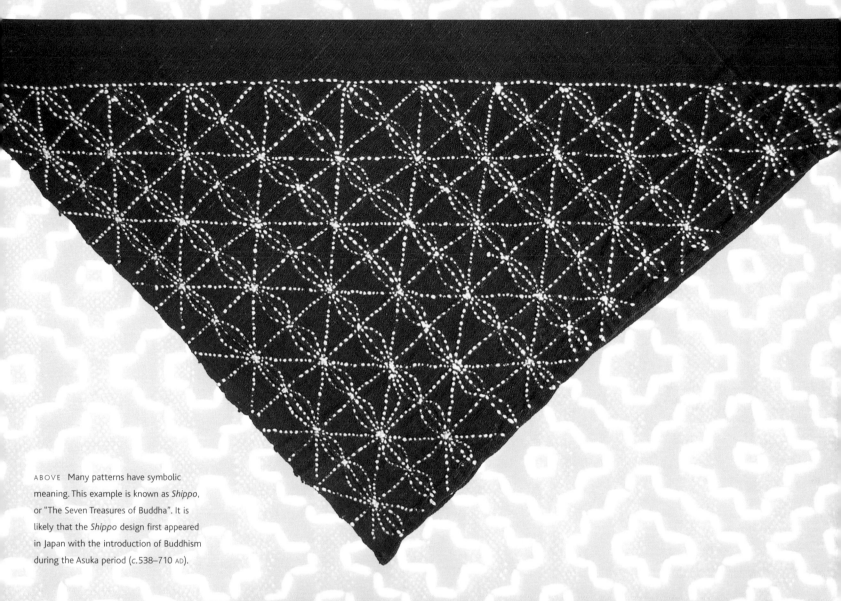

ABOVE Many patterns have symbolic meaning. This example is known as *Shippo*, or "The Seven Treasures of Buddha". It is likely that the *Shippo* design first appeared in Japan with the introduction of Buddhism during the Asuka period (*c.*538–710 AD).

RIGHT On the left of the picture is the *Asanoha*, or "Hemp Leaf", one of the most popular of all *sashiko* designs. Paintings from the Heian period (794–1185) often show the Buddha clothed in fabric patterned with this design. In modern Japan, *Asanoha* is often used on clothing for babies and small children, conveying the wish that the child will grow as vigorously as the perennial hemp plant. The pattern on the right is an overlaid check pattern, known as *Kosh*; in this instance it is combined with *shibori*, a tie-dye technique (*see* page 30).

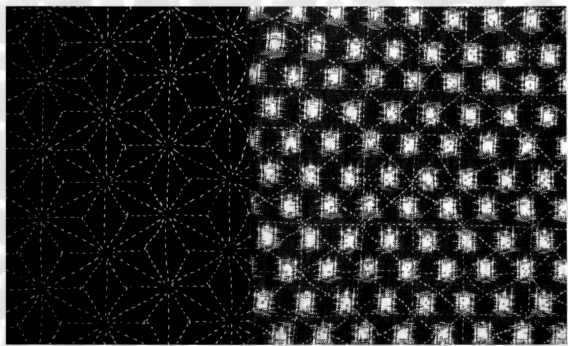

16TH-CENTURY PATCHWORK

The crazy patchwork style known as *yosegire* is thought of as a 16th-century technique largely because of the existence of some particularly fine examples from that period. Perhaps the most notable of these is the wonderful *dofuku* robe, a patchwork coat that was made for the famous Japanese general Uesugi Kenshin in about 1560. Garments patched from rich and expensive fabrics were everyday wear for the aristocracy, demonstrating the importance to the Japanese of prolonging the life of old and precious textiles. It was considered appropriate that the number of patches in such a garment, presented to a loved or respected superior, should match the age of the recipient – especially on auspicious birthdays such as 77, 88, and 99. The coat illustrated here is an exceptionally fine expression of the philosophical and spiritual symbolism underlying the Japanese attitude to patchwork. It was a gift to Uesugi Kenshin from a warlord whom he had served, and contains 17 rare and expensive Chinese brocades, many woven with gold and silver threads. If the number of patches represents Kenshin's age then he must have lived to be very old – it contains over a hundred!

RIGHT The famous coat worn by Uesugi Kenshin. The individual patches are outlined with fine gold cord couched over the seams. This fabulous garment would have been a worthy gift for a hero, even by the standards of the time, when highly prized fabrics were everyday wear in the higher reaches of society.

16TH-CENTURY PATCHWORK: METHOD AND STYLE

Patchwork in this traditional style lends itself beautifully to contemporary interpretation and use. An eclectic range of fabrics can be included, such as cottons, silks, satins, and brocades, and these can be pieced together either as quilts or as yardage for garments. In the examples pictured, strips of fabric 10cm (4in) wide have been cut into squares, rectangles, triangles, parallelograms, and trapezoids. To cut two patches to be sewn together by a diagonal seam, lay them end-to-end, both right-side-up, on the cutting board. Move one strip on top of the other and use ruler and cutter to cut a diagonal line through both fabrics, then join the patches right sides together. The shaped patches are sewn together to make long strips, which are then seamed together, side-by-side. The patchwork is used with the strips running vertically.

LEFT Detail of a padded and quilted dressing-gown by Celia Eddy. Made as a gift to welcome the maker's son-in-law into the family, this contemporary *yosegire* patchwork reflects the spirit and meaning embodied in those garments made traditionally in this style. With this style of patchwork, more patches can be added whenever repairs are needed without detracting from the overall effect — a great advantage for garments that receive regular wear.

RIGHT Detail of "Yosegire Blues for Vaseema" by Celia Eddy. The fabrics are an eclectic selection of silks, satins, brocades, and cottons. Seams of the individual patches are embellished with machine stitching, while red satin ribbon has been couched over the long joining strips. The patchwork is made up in sections to fit each of the pattern pieces. Each section is then basted onto thin batting and backing fabric and machine-quilted along the seams. The sections are joined and the garment is completed by the addition of facings and lining.

INDIGO QUILTS

LEFT "Dream Windows" (detail) by Shizuko Kuroha, 2001, machine-pieced and hand-quilted. This variation on the "Log Cabin" style of patchwork incorporates many Japanese indigo-dyed fabrics. In fact, it could be described as a sampler of Japanese indigo patterns. Many contemporary Japanese quiltmakers refer to their textile craft heritage in their work by including Japanese fabrics.

Indigo dye has been used to colour cloth blue for thousands of years. In Japan it was obtained from the polygonum plant (*Polygonum tinctorium*) and was used to dye the cotton clothing of farmers, fishermen, merchants, and artisans, who were not allowed to wear patterned silks and brocades because these were restricted to the ruling classes. Ever inventive, the indigo dyers developed the art of *shibori* ("shaped resist dyeing", such as tie-dyeing), and the town of Arimatsu, in western Aichi, still produces traditional *shibori*-dyed cloth to this day.

When Japanese quiltmakers were first exposed to the traditions of American quiltmaking during the 1970s their first instinct was to use the indigenous indigo-dyed fabrics. As a result there are many beautiful quilts made during the latter part of the 20th century containing mostly indigo fabrics. The unique colour and properties of this ancient dye, coupled with the *shibori* technique, continue to inspire quiltmakers not only in Japan but also the world over. These blue quilts have a unique luminosity that outshines those containing chemically dyed fabrics.

RIGHT "Indigo Tapestry" by Noriko Kuroda. Noriko has been collecting indigo fabrics for years; she makes her quilts to "let them live again", as she says. This is a characteristically Japanese interpretation of American patchwork, in which small patches of squares and rectangles are set with octagons, each of which highlights a carefully selected patterned fabric.

"A Variety of New Year Dreams" by Setsuko Obi, 2004. Various patches have pictures, words, and letters to recall happy New Year dreams. Both English and Japanese references are included. The quilt, made from colourful woven silk, is pieced in blocks separated by a 1cm (⅜in) lattice. The intricated piecing and brilliant gradation of colour are hallmarks of this artist's work.

"The Tale of Genji" by Reiko Domon, 2004. Made from the silks of kimonos worn by the artist's mother and grandmother, this quilt was inspired by the novel written by Lady Murasaki during the Heian era (794–1185), which is generally acknowledged to be the first novel ever written. Genji was born into the lower ranks of the court but achieved fame for his music and poetry, as well as notoriety for his scandalous amatory adventures! Reiko Domon comments: "I hoped to express the hearts of the ladies in the story." The deep pink silk with the flower pattern came from a kimono that her mother wore during the Taisho era.

KOREA : HISTORY AND TRADITIONS

"Every traditional pojagi *which survives today is treasured as a unique expression of the character of the nameless woman who created it."* Huh Dong-hwa, *Rapt in Color: Korean Textiles and Costumes of the Choson Dynasty*

WRAPPING CLOTHS

Among the most celebrated artistic endeavours in Korean history are the magnificent costumes and wrapping cloths created exclusively by women, most of them during the Choson dynasty (1392–1910). Wrapping cloths are a feature of many Asian cultures: they are found in India and Japan, and among many other countries of the region. However, nowhere have they occupied a more prominent place in the everyday life of the community than in Korea, where they are called *pojagi*.

Pojagi are functional – they are used to wrap, carry, and cover all manner of things, from food to gifts – but they also have symbolic meaning. They serve as an expression of respect, not only for the items that they cover, but also for the recipient of a gift. The techniques used to create and embellish the cloths include embroidery, patchwork, and quilting. Some *pojagi* have become treasured heirlooms, handed down from generation to generation. Their value lies not only in their exquisite needlework but also in their embodiment of folk belief: patterns in *pojagi* symbolize the pursuit of happiness and good fortune.

CHOGAK PO

Traditional *pojagi* are classified in various ways according to their use, the status of the user, their design, and composition. For example, the wrapping cloths used by royalty are called *kung po*, while *min po* are used by ordinary folk. And among the many dazzling artifacts within this rich tradition, none is more remarkable than the patchwork and quilted wrapping cloths known as *chogak po*. They belong to a culture in which, throughout the history of Korea, the production of fabrics and the cutting, sewing, and embellishment of clothes and many other domestic items was women's work.

The surviving examples of *chogak po* made during the Choson dynasty serve to illustrate the creative talents of the unknown Korean women of the time. These women lived in an extremely rigid society, but

LEFT A 19th-century patchwork wrapping cloth pieced from pastel-coloured silks. Designs of this "network" type – here an abstract expression of water rings – are thought to have the symbolic power to invite happiness and to guard against misfortune, because devils become ensnared in the net.

RIGHT A 19th-century embroidered cloth from the eastern province of Korea, featuring abstract images of trees and a pair of dancing birds in the centre. It was used as a wrapping cloth for family gifts at a wedding.

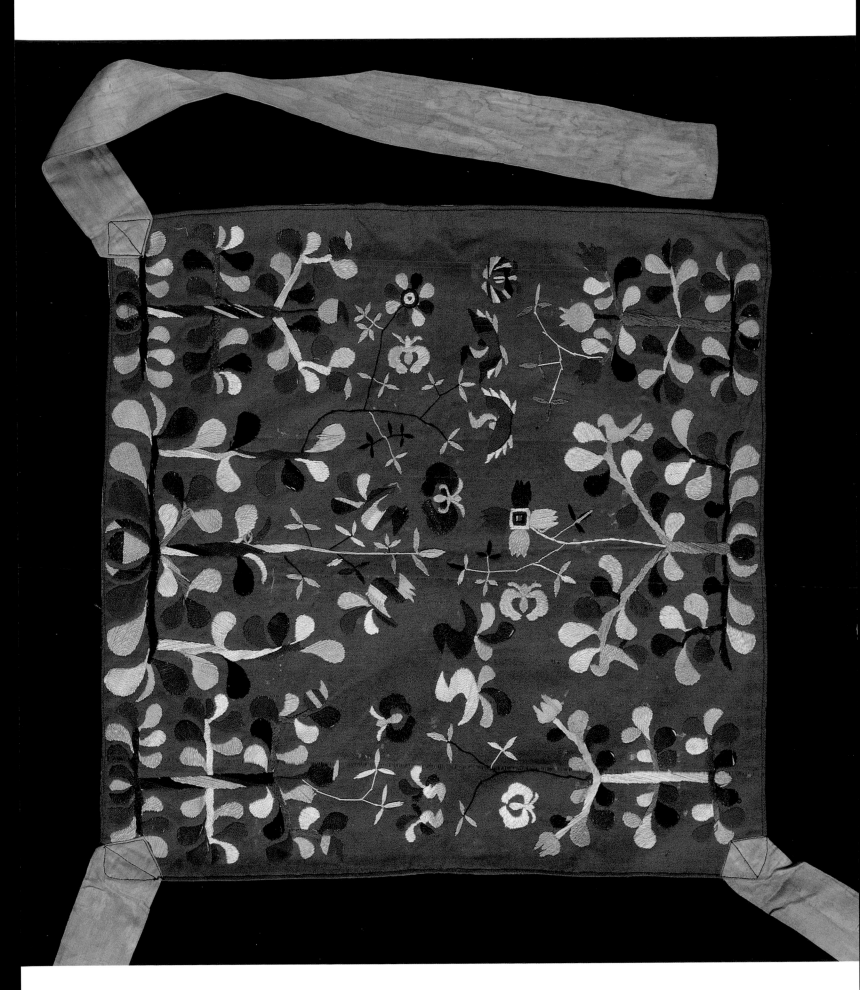

their clear delight in this creative activity is revealed in the exuberant colours and designs of their patchwork and embroidery. Perhaps this was a way of discovering and expressing gifts and talents that might otherwise have had no outlet.

The *chogak po* patchwork is a mosaic of cloth made from scraps of leftover material. Thin, loosely woven silk versions were used in the summer months to protect food from flies and dust, while the quilted and lined cloths kept food warm in winter. The most distinctive feature of

these cloths is their harmonious use of colour; each colour scheme is a unique reflection of the personality and creative imagination of the maker.

Most *chogak po* are pieced in an organized pattern, such as chequerboards, triangles, and framed squares, but others are an elaborate joining of odd scraps of cloth, closely resembling the Western style known as "crazy" patchwork (*see* pages 62–5). They are sometimes tied with bat-shaped knots to bring good luck, as bats were believed to drive away evil spirits.

LEFT *Chogak po* dating from the mid-19th century. The small, bat-shaped knots in the four corners of the inner square both anchor the patchwork to its lining and have talismanic significance. *Chogak po* of this style were used mostly as table or food coverings.

ABOVE A 19th-century *chogak po* pieced from remnants of silk recycled from dress-making fabrics. This example was used as a table cover to protect food from insects and dust.

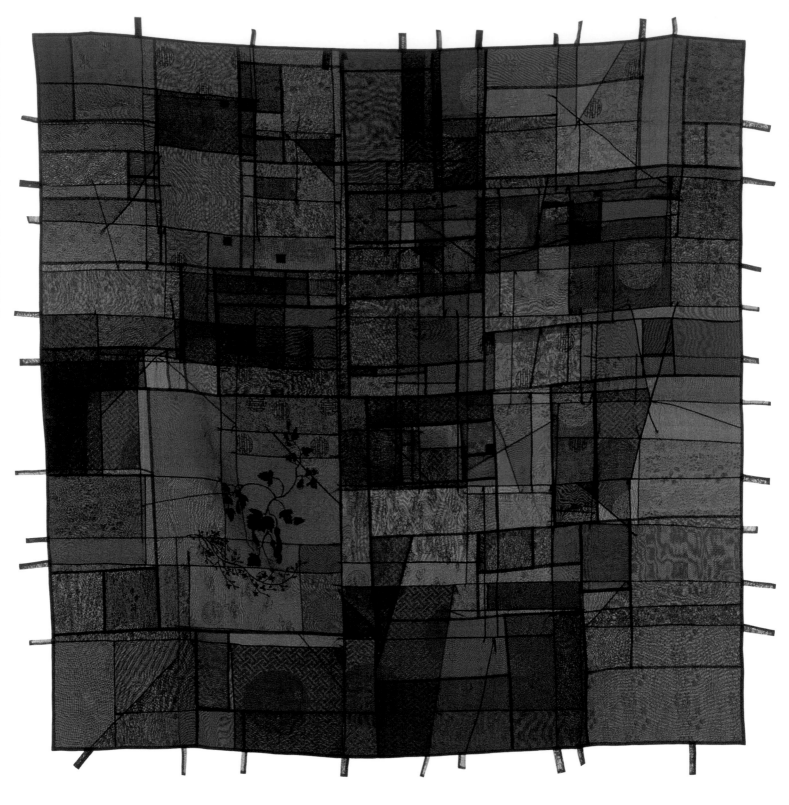

"No-name Women '04" *pojagi* **by Chunghie Lee, 2004.** The artist pays tribute to the generations of anonymous Korean women who, unsung and undervalued, worked within the boundaries of a traditional craft to create exquisite works of textile art. Lee remarks that they lived their lives faithfully, and did not "eat the rice of idleness" – working for their families from early morning to late in the day. Carefully they saved scraps of precious fabrics, then played with shapes and colours to create *pojagi* that, uninfluenced by trends or fashions, manage to achieve true artistry.

"The Wall" by Misik Kim, 2002. The fabrics are all hand-dyed and hand-quilted by the artist, and the techniques used include machine-piecing and appliqué. In this quilt, symbolic reference is made to the many walls that surround us throughout life – both the visible and the invisible. However, walls are not just barriers – they can represent security and warmth, too.

INDIA: HISTORY AND TRADITIONS

Quiltmaking in India has a long history; the quilts sent back to Europe by European traders from early in the 17th century illustrate skills and traditions that were already hundreds of years old.

CHINTZES

For centuries before the arrival in India of those first Europeans, Indian chintzes and the famous double-ikat silks of Gujarat were highly prized in many parts of the ancient world, and dominated the textile markets of Asia. Archeological evidence from Egypt dates this tradition from at least the 9th century AD. Indian crafts-men had achieved a unique mastery of the processes that went into the production of these textiles: weaving, dyeing, designing, printing, and painting were all highly developed, which assured the production of the uniquely beautiful, brightly patterned cloths known as chintzes. The European traders arriving in the early 17th century were quick to recognize the potential market in Europe for these exotic cloths, and it was not long before a huge demand was created for them. Bolts of cloth were exported to be made up into garments, curtains, bed hangings, and furnishings of every sort; Samuel Pepys, in his diary for 1663, notes that he has bought his wife "a chint (sic) that is a painted calico for to line her new study which is very preetie" (sic), and also that he has purchased "an Indian gown for myself".

These chintz fabrics were expensive and therefore precious, which accounts for the fact that they appear frequently in European quilts and patchwork, as even the smallest scraps would not be wasted. For example, the famous Levens Hall bed furnishings (*see* pages 54–5), consisting of a quilt and bed curtains, were pieced from imported Indian chintzes, and there are many surviving examples found in *broderie perse* (quilts with cut-out motifs on a background). But it was not only bolts of fabric that were exported to Europe: quilts made from the renowned chintz were also in demand. One important source of information about the import of chintz quilts exists in the records kept by the Dutch East India Company. Throughout the 17th century, ships' manifests listed "stitched/padded Bengal quilts". In 1641, for example, 36 items of this sort were recorded, and by 1658 no fewer than 200 were listed. Some of the finest examples of imported Indian quilts, usually wholecloth rather than pieced, and dating from the early 18th century, are in the Netherlands Open-Air Museum in Arnhem. However, these quilts were almost certainly made especially for the European export trade; they bear little resemblance to the ethnic and tribal quilted artifacts that were, and remain, a strong and vibrant feature throughout the Indus region of the Indian subcontinent.

LEFT This unusual Indian chintz quilt from the Coromandel Coast was made between 1700 and 1725 and is a magnificent example of the sort of quilt exported to Holland and other European countries during the 18th century. It has a centre medallion, corner ornaments, and in-fill patterns of flowering stems, feathers, and birds, while the red border has a pattern of grotesques. It is padded with wool and silk and quilted with silk thread. The quilt is lined with green silk, which reveals the exceedingly fine quality of the quilting.

RIGHT A magnificent Indian chintz quilt in a traditional "Tree of Life" design. It is from around 1720 and is another quilt exported to Holland. The border is 40cm (16in) wide and has a winding branch and flowers. The quilt is backed in cream-coloured silk and the quilting over the entire piece follows the pattern of the chintz on the top, which, as it is so elaborate, makes it difficult to "read" the quilting pattern on the back.

RALLIS

LEFT *Ralli* made in Sindh, Pakistan, in the mid-20th century. The design of arrowheads pointing in opposite directions is one of the most popular patchwork patterns from this region. Its origins can be traced back to patterns found on pottery from the Indus Valley (*c.*2000 BC), and, coincidentally, it is also reminiscent of the American "Flying Geese" pattern.

RIGHT *Ralli* belonging to one of the ruling families of Hyderabad, Sindh, early 20th century. This is a virtuoso quilt featuring folded and cut appliqué in 12 patterns. Appliqué quilts are often named according to the number of blocks they have, so this is a "12 block ralli".

"*Every* ralli *quilt tells a story. It tells of the natural creativity and love of color and design of the women who create them. [It] tells the story of the strength of tradition. The basic designs and motifs of* rallis *have been passed from mother to daughter and woman to woman for maybe thousands of years.*" Patricia Ormsby Stoddard, *Ralli Quilts*

Patchwork, appliqué, and embroidered quilts made in the Indus region of the Indian subcontinent are among the most vibrant in the world – rich with colour and embellishment. The name *ralli* originates from the local word meaning "to mix", or "to connect". They are made by both Muslim and Hindu women from many tribes and castes, in towns, villages, and among nomadic tribes.

Some of the most distinctive quilts belong to the people of the Kutch region, whose way of life is still basically tribal despite the encroaching influence of the outside world. Daily life is dominated by ritual, and decorative textiles, especially clothes and quilts, play an important role in maintaining a sense of cultural identity and continuity. The dowry system is still in use, and quilts, bags, and pillows are essential elements of this.

KANTHAS

The fine needlework quilts known as *kantha* in Bangladesh and *sujuni* in Bihar are unique examples of women's folk art – a distinctive marriage of quilting and embroidery. There are many regional variations in style and technique because, like many craft traditions, they have evolved from a combination of economic circumstance and practical need, to which were added the artistic skills and imagination of the makers. *Kanthas* were used as quilts in the cooler weather, as floor mats, and as covers and wrapping cloths for books and other valuables. In the past they were made from worn-out clothing such as saris and *dhotis* (loose white cotton garments worn by men), for family use or as gifts.

By the 1970s the making of high-quality traditional *kanthas* had fallen into decline, but since then there has been a remarkable revival, largely thanks to the role of organizations dedicated to fostering improvement in the conditions of women in rural areas. This has resulted in some changes in the styles of *kantha* produced, to make them more marketable; but, as Niaz Zaman has observed, "...there is an endeavour to create a lost tradition where art and craft blend into one indistinguishable whole".

ABOVE *Kantha* from Bengal, 19th century. An exceptionally fine *kantha* with a stylized lotus, a symbol of life, as the central motif. This is surrounded by a wealth of figures drawn from the ranks of 19th-century Calcutta nobility, and includes Europeans playing cards as well as depictions of local people and activities.

RIGHT A classic "mirror image" Tree of Life *kantha* from Bengal, c.1900. The "Tree of Life" motif is popular in agrarian societies, where nature plays such an important role and where it is seen as a symbol of fertility. The border motifs are based on *alpana*, ritual drawings made on the ground with a paste of rice flour.

KANTHAS: METHOD AND STYLE

Traditional *kanthas* were made by layering old saris and *dhotis*, which were very soft and therefore easy to sew through several layers. The layers of cloth were smoothed, usually by spreading them on the ground and placing weights on the edges. These were then carefully folded in and stitched, and two or three rows of tacking stitches sewn down the length of the *kantha*. The women sat on the ground and worked without hoops or frames. The motifs were first outlined with a needle and thread, then filled in with variations of running stitches.

RIGHT Early quilts were sewn with simple running stitches, and these stitches were also used to embellish the quilts with motifs drawn from a rich cultural life, many of which, such as the lotus, the sun, and the "Tree of Life", are found in other cultures too.

BELOW *Kantha* motifs often relate specifically to the local environment; in images of nature, as well as domestic and agricultural activities and implements, a woman was stitching into her quilts the everyday life around her. Animals, therefore, often feature in *kanthas*, and many of them have acquired symbolic meaning; the elephant, for example, represents material prosperity. Here, the main figure has first been outlined then filled in with rows of a characteristic *kantha* stitch, which creates a ripple effect.

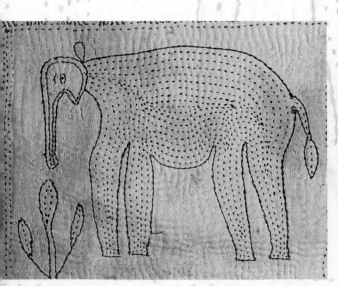

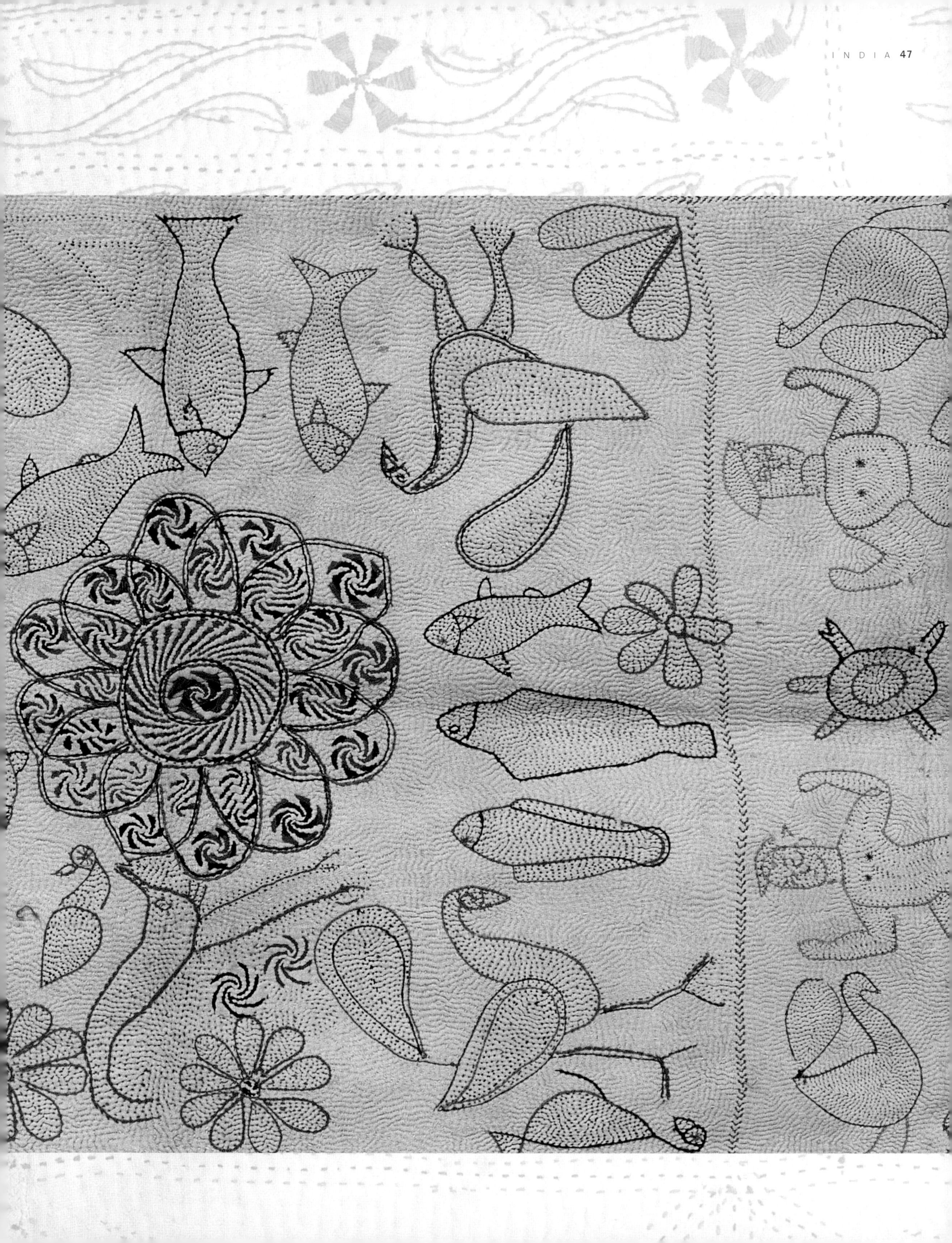

SUJUNIS OF BIHAR

The quilts made in Bihar are known as *sujuni* and, like the *kanthas* of Bangladesh, are a combination of embroidery and quilting. They are made as gifts for family celebrations such as weddings or births. Women traditionally make *sujuni* at home, laying worn-out saris on top of each other, stitching them with coloured threads, and embroidering into them scenes from village life.

Sujunis are made by both Hindu and Muslim women in Bihar – a part of India that suffers from extreme inequality and poverty. In 1988 an income-generation programme was started by an NGO (Non-Governmental Organization) to work with women and girls in rural areas. The programme now works with thousands throughout the state, enabling them to generate some income from their traditional skills. The basic aim of the Organization is to enable women who traditionally have remained poor and subordinated to gain some control over their own lives, to have access to education, and to improve their economic status.

However, rather than simply making copies of traditional *sujunis* to sell to tourists – the fate suffered by many ethnic textile traditions – the women preserve the continuity of their culture by depicting their own lives and circumstances on the quilts. Through their stitching they not only record the activities and events of village life, such as festivals and weddings, but they also make personal observations on current concerns such as education, women's work, nature, and the environment.

ABOVE "New York" *sujuni*, made in Bihar, c.1998. This embroidered *sujuni* depicts the artist's visit to New York: included are the Statue of Liberty, cruise boats, the subway, skyscrapers, and the World Trade Center. The young artist was much impressed by the number of women driving vehicles, so they are also shown!

RIGHT "Women and Work" *sujuni*, made in Bihar, 2002. Another embroidered *sujuni*, from the ADITHI co-operative, depicting the everyday lives of the makers: housework, cooking, market trading, making offerings and worshipping at the temple, and managing the fish in the lake. The border shows girls going to school.

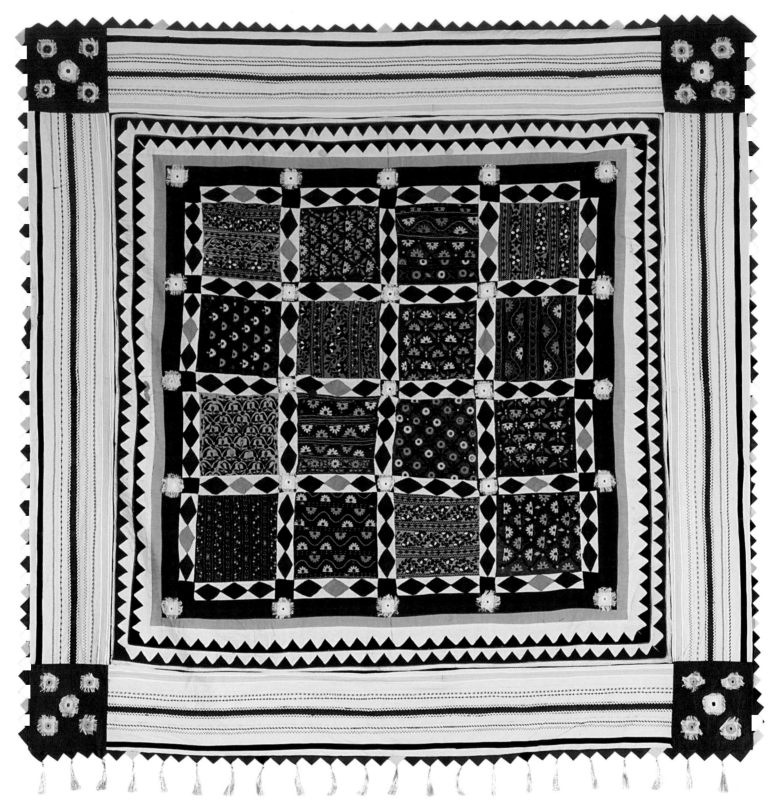

"Shimmering Colours from India" by Ranbir Kaur, 2004. This is made using Indian cotton threads, machine-pieced and embellished with *shisha* mirrors and hand embroidery. To this artist, whose roots are in India but who now lives in the UK, Indian textile designs are a continuous source of inspiration. The centrefield is an interpretation of a traditional *ralli*-style quilt, using the hot colours and embellishment reminiscent of such quilts. The centrefield is surrounded by borders and the bottom of the quilt is finished with tassels.

"Paradise?" by Lynn Setterington, 2003. The artist has been inspired for some years by the ideas and techniques involved in *kantha*-making. In the spirit of the traditional *kantha*-makers, her quilts reflect the interests and concerns of her own life. In this quilt, the floral fabric refers to a modern *kantha* in which a patterned cloth had been included in the layered fabrics and unintentionally showed through the top cloth. Another underlying theme in this quilt is that of the gardens depicted in Persian carpets, which, in turn, links to the idea of Paradise as a garden.

THE EUROPEAN CONTRIBUTION TO THE ILLUSTRIOUS

HISTORY OF THE QUILT BEGINS WITH THE FABULOUSLY

WORKED SICILIAN QUILT OF THE LATE-14TH CENTURY,

AND REACHES ITS ZENITH WITH THE EXPORT TO

THE NEW WORLD OF ITS ACCUMULATED TREASURY OF

NEEDLECRAFT SKILLS AND TRADITIONS. PATCHWORK

EUROPE

AND QUILTING IN EUROPE MAY NOT HAVE CARRIED

THE WEIGHT OF TALISMANIC AND SYMBOLIC MEANING

THAT THEY BORE IN MUCH OF ASIA AND AFRICA, BUT

THEY MADE A RICH AND DIVERSE CONTRIBUTION TO

THE DOMESTIC SCENE, PARTICULARLY IN CLOTHES AND

BEDDING, AND TO THE CHURCH IN THE FORM OF

VESTMENTS FOR CEREMONIAL USE.

ENGLAND : HISTORY AND TRADITIONS

Patchwork and quilting have become so firmly associated with each other in the past hundred years that it is often forgotten that they are two distinct crafts, each with a separate history and tradition. Nowhere is this more true than in the British Isles, where early patchwork was often unquilted, and wholecloth quilts, with their emphasis on quilting pattern, developed their own identity. In England, examples of exquisite quilting applied to many garments, including petticoats, coats, and babies' bonnets, survive from the 18th century. It is likely that they are the work of professional embroiderers, who would probably have been members of an embroiderers' guild.

In rural areas quilting was a thriving cottage industry, producing warm and serviceable bed coverings for cold winters. Strong and more artistic traditions grew up in the north east (Durham and Northumberland), and men and women who earned a living as quilters were to be found in both rural and more populated areas.

PATCHWORK

Patchwork as a distinct but complementary craft has had its own history. Since thrift has always been a motivation for making patchwork, it has at times been denigrated for its associations with poverty. Indeed, much patchwork would have been made from fabrics that had already seen hard wear, which no doubt accounts for the fact that so few early examples survive.

Despite its associations with the "make do and mend" philosophy of the less affluent, patchwork was not made only in that context. Early surviving examples include a silk coverlet dated 1718 (*see* page 12), pieced from luxurious silks. Another remarkable example of patchwork, believed to date from 1708, is a set of bed hangings (right) and a quilt, at Levens Hall in Cumbria, pieced from imported chintzes. Even tiny pieces of the printed cotton have been used, reflecting the value put on imported Indian fabrics before the development of a calico printing industry in Europe.

PREVIOUS PAGE Detail of "The Story of Tristram", one of three corded and stuffed Sicilian quilts dating from around 1359, worked in all-white linen with cotton fillings. The piece, which may have been made as a wall hanging or bed cover, narrates the legend of Tristram, a hero of 12th-century troubadour poetry. The story is told in a series of panels containing both figurative images and lettering, and the superb workmanship indicates that by the time this quilt was made quilting was a widespread and highly developed technique in Europe.

RIGHT Detail from a set of patchwork bed furnishings found at Levens Hall in Cumbria, c.1708, comprising a bed quilt and bed curtains. They are believed to be the earliest surviving examples of English patchwork. Although there is no documentation to support its provenance, circumstantial evidence suggests that it was made by the wife and daughters of the family who lived at the hall at that time. The patchwork design is pieced from octagons, cross shapes, and long hexagons in the sort of imported printed cottons that were highly fashionable during the 17th and 18th centuries. The patchwork was pieced over papers in the traditional English style, using very fine stitches and linen thread.

LEFT A superb quilted travelling costume, c.1745–60. It comprises a petticoat with a short, hooded jacket, which has rounded box pleats at the back and a bodice fastened with hooks and eyes. The sleeves are fitted to the elbow and finished with deep ruffles. The outfit is densely quilted all over with a rich profusion of patterns. Work of this quality was probably executed by professionals, and the variation in the stitching suggests that it is the work of more than one person.

LEFT "High Summer" by Averil Colby, completed in 1951. This cotton coverlet, in an unconventional pattern for its time, is pieced entirely in hexagons made of 19th-and 20th-century floral chintzes. Fabric for each hexagon has been skilfully selected and positioned to build up the wreaths of summer roses, so that it is difficult to believe that the pattern is actually created entirely from hexagons.

RIGHT "The Keyboard Patchwork" by Lucy Boston, probably started in 1967 when Lucy was 75. The patchwork may have been inspired by a Devonshire quilt c.1870 illustrated in Averil Colby's Patchwork, but her interpretation of the pattern is remarkable as it contains 154 blocks, each one built up from carefully selected patterned fabrics and surrounded by white octagons.

AVERIL COLBY AND HER LEGACY

Although interest in patchwork and quilting had declined by the early 20th century, for some women it never lost its fascination. One of the most notable of these was Averil Colby (1900–82). Not only was she a prolific and skilled practitioner, she was also the chronicler of British quilting and patchwork traditions in her books Patchwork (1958) and Quilting (1972). Both her books and her patchwork quilts have had a profound influence on succeeding generations of hobbyists and professional quilt artists.

Many of today's patchworkers will remember first learning "Grandmother's Garden" – the joining together of hexagons in a pattern – which has consequently come to be regarded as rather dull. However, Averil Colby used it with rare artistry, skilfully combining patterned fabrics to build up complex and sophisticated patterns, and thus proving that even the simplest techniques can produce highly aesthetic and refined work.

This approach to patchwork is wonderfully apparent in the work of another 20th-century patchworker, Lucy Boston (1892–1990), whose outstanding skills as a patchworker matched her more celebrated abilities as writer and gardener. Working long before the advent of quilting shops and patchwork fabrics, Lucy Boston used her artistic eye to select and combine fabrics and shapes to produce a series of outstanding patchworks.

ENGLISH MOSAIC PATCHWORK

The technique of making patchwork over paper templates has come to be known as "English patchwork". It is an easy way of creating complex geometrical patterns of the sort found in traditional mosaics – for instance, on tiled floors and in parquetry – and so it is also known as "mosaic patchwork". Patterns built up in this way are known as "all-over" designs, as opposed to patchwork organized in a series of frames or in blocks, both of which were common techniques in British quilting. These "all-over" designs became most popular from the Victorian era onward, when the patterns would have been seen everywhere in houses and institutional buildings, especially in floor tiles, and would naturally have been appropriated for use in patchwork.

Although English mosaic patchwork is normally associated with the use of hexagons, the documentation of British quilts made in the early 1990s by the Quilters' Guild of the British Isles revealed that many other tessellating geometric shapes, including diamonds, octagons with squares, squares, rectangles, and triangles of many sizes, were also common. Today much piecing is done by machine, but this more leisurely and easily transportable hand-sewn method retains its popularity.

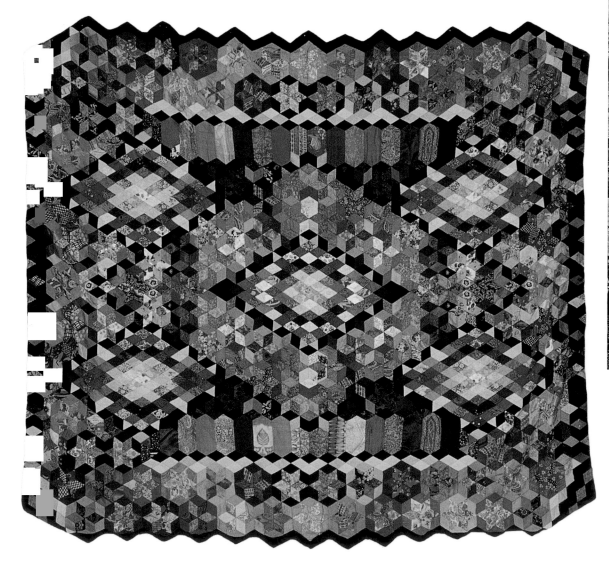

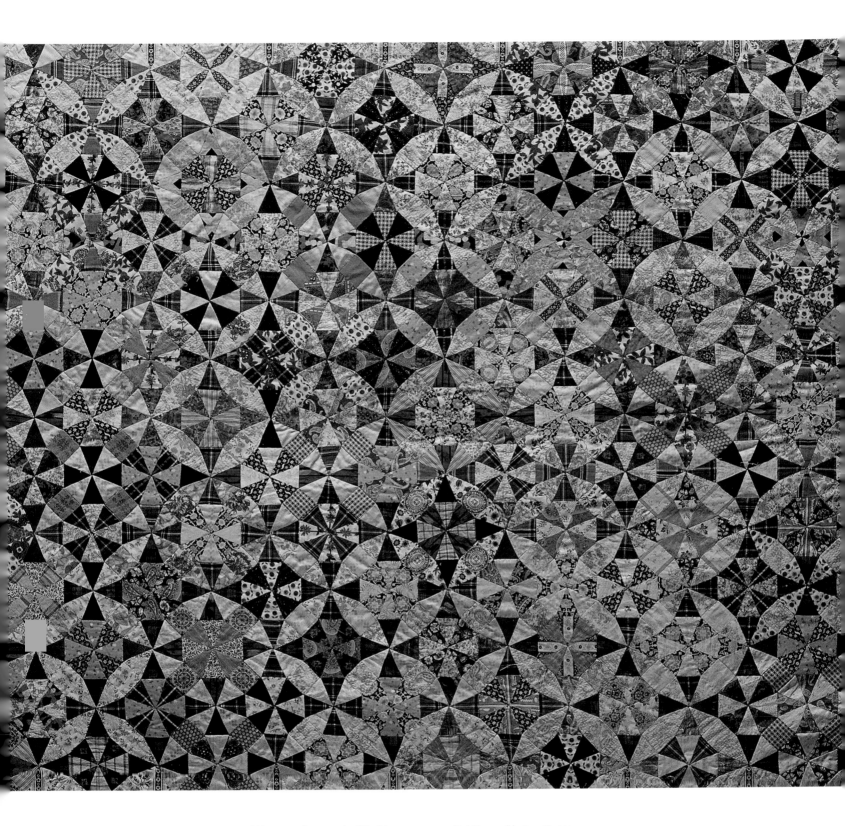

LEFT This outstanding example of English mosaic piecing was made as a wedding quilt in 1934 by Edith Young and Isabel Aspinall on the Isle of Man. It contains fabric from family dresses dating back to 1860, and therefore serves as an archive of dress fabrics over a long period of time. It is pieced in long hexagons and Tumbling Blocks, and contains 2,600 pieces in total.

ABOVE "Kaleidoscope" by Lucy Boston, 1974. A traditional American design pieced in the English style over papers. This is a brilliant interpretation of a design that, although it involves only straight lines, creates the illusion of stars set in overlapping circles. For each patch, exactly the right colour and pattern of fabric had to be chosen to create an iridescent surface.

ENGLISH MOSAIC PATCHWORK: METHOD AND STYLE

To make patchwork by this method a master template for each shape is needed, usually made of card or metal, although ready-made acrylic templates can be bought nowadays. This is drawn round to make paper templates, one for each patch needed. The fabric patch is cut with a seam allowance which is then tacked over the paper, using the edge of the paper as a guide. The patches are then placed right sides together and stitched to each other by sewing across the seams with small stitches. When the patchwork is complete the tacking stitches are removed and the papers can be taken out.

LEFT Reverse side of an unfinished patchwork coverlet, c.1860–70, made by an elderly countrywoman in Northumberland. Small hexagons are pieced to form larger hexagons, all with the original papers and tacking stitches still in place. Some of the papers are dated as early as 1841 and 1855; papers found in old patchworks often provide useful information about dates and provenance.

RIGHT This "Tumbling Blocks" coverlet, c.1900, is from Ravenglass in Cumbria. It is made in brilliant multicoloured silks and mainly features black and yellow but it incorporates many other colours too. This is a superb example of the English patchwork style, creating an overall pattern with a glowing, jewel-like effect.

VICTORIAN CRAZY PATCHWORK

Before Victorian times, crazy patchwork was simply utilitarian, the product of poverty: remnants of fabric would be stitched together randomly to provide warm bedding. However, from the second half of the 19th century onward the style was adopted by more affluent households and became very popular as an activity for genteel women with time on their hands. Crazy patchwork was not only used for bed coverings but could also be found on chair throws, table covers, bags, and many other domestic items, such as tea cosies and cushions.

The patchwork was built up by stitching random patches of mixed fabrics onto a foundation. The fabrics often incorporated the silks, satins, and velvets that were fashionable in the clothing of the period, and resulted in a complicated, multicoloured surface. Some people considered this style of patchwork to be the height of bad taste, partly because the embellishments with which it was usually covered were often quite garish. The vogue for crazy patchwork was not confined to the British Isles but also became very popular in the USA and Australia.

LEFT Crazy patchwork quilt in mixed fabrics, dated 1887. An inscription in one corner reads: "Mother, 63 Years". This is an example of patches selected completely at random and assembled over the whole quilt to make a complex surface. It is embellished with embroidered flowers and fancy stitches over the seams.

ABOVE Sparkling sequins, buttons, and beads catch the eye in this extremely ornate velvet and silk quilt. There are nine blocks surrounded by a narrow border, then a wider border of more blocks of crazy patchwork. The corner blocks are heavily embellished eight-pointed stars. The patches are edged with embroidery and appliqué shapes.

VICTORIAN CRAZY PATCHWORK: METHOD AND STYLE

At the height of its popularity crazy patchwork was used for all manner of items, from chair and table throws to cushions and tea cosies. In many cases it comprised remnants of fabrics used for dresses and other garments, including bright silks, satins, and velvets seen in evening gowns of the Victorian period. This, to a large extent, accounts for the rich and glowing surface of much surviving 19th-century patchwork. The vogue for crazy patchwork has been attributed, variously, to the popularity of Japanese *yosegire* patchwork (*see* pages 26–9) and of Chinese porcelain "crackle" glaze, characterized by its fine crazing.

ABOVE The crazy patchwork shown above is pieced in a variety of silk, cotton, and velvet fabrics, and displays a wide range of embroidery stitches and patterns, including feather stitch, cross stitch, and chain stitch. A harp and what appears to be a five-barred gate appear, so perhaps these objects had special significance for the maker. The name "Alice Wall" is on one of the patches but it is not known for sure whether it is her work.

RIGHT This detail highlights the exquisite embroidery that so often appears on Victorian crazy patchwork. Embroidery, braids, and couching have been used on the seams. Stitches used include beautifully worked and unusual embroidery stitches, such as "Closed Herringbone", "Double Feather Stitch", and "Fly Stitch".

"My Paradise Garden" by Anne Hulbert. This is a lively contemporary interpretation of crazy patchwork based on a gardening theme. It is pieced from a wide range of randomly cut patches of various silks stitched to a calico foundation, and is hand-embroidered with silk and metallic threads. The embellishment includes appliqué, quilting, ribbon embroidery, trapunto, and beadwork, and among the garden motifs are butterflies, a spider's web, grapes, leaves, a snail, and a bird eating berries.

"Emmeshes VII Sunshine and Shadow" by Sally-Ann Boyd. In an imaginative interpretation of the crazy patchwork style, the artist has used pieces of fabric that are too small for the Seminole and strip patchwork that she usually makes. She has stitched the pieces into 10cm (4in) crazy patchwork squares and has arranged them in alternating rounds in bright then sombre fabrics, in the traditional "Sunshine and Shadows" pattern.

NORTH COUNTRY QUILTS

LEFT "Triple X" pieced quilt, c.1910. Although the maker of this quilt is unknown, it is thought to have come from Castleside in Co. Durham. The design was probably marked out by a professional quilt designer; the fabric is yellow and cream cotton sateen, with a flowered furnishing cotton on the reverse. The quilting patterns include "Rose in a Ring" in the first border and a "Cable Twist" in the outer border. "Freehand Feathers", "Small Feather", and "Weardale Chain" are also used.

RIGHT "Framed Centre Medallion" coverlet made by Martha Jackson in Westmoreland, c.1790–5. This patchwork coverlet is made from printed and white cottons, pieced and appliquéd. Although unfinished, with no backing, it is a superb example of the English frame style. The four centre blocks are appliquéd with flowers and tendrils, while the first frame is pieced entirely from hexagons. The next frame echoes the pattern surrounding each of the centre blocks, while a final frame is pieced from squares "on point".

"Vitality and charm are the essence of the best quilts from this era..." Dorothy Ostler, *North Country Quilts: Legend and Living Tradition*

The late 19th to the early 20th century has been described as a "Golden Age" of North Country quiltmaking, when wholecloth, frame, pieced, and appliqué quilts were made in great numbers. This may be because particular patterns and designs acquired regional associations, so that quiltmaking became a popular way of expressing regional identity. North Country quilts emerged from a very particular social and economic context, in which quilt-making was a strong tradition based in both family and community life. Families and friends would quilt together, and social gatherings combined quiltmaking with music, singing, and dancing. Both pieced and wholecloth quilts are held in high regard for their craftsmanship and beauty, but the wholecloth quilts best reveal the distinctive patterns of the region. Social and economic change after World War II meant that quilting almost died out, but a few people kept the tradition alive, most notably Amy Emms (1904–98), whose enthusiasm and teaching skills ensured that the old craft traditions were perpetuated.

NORTH COUNTRY QUILTS: METHOD AND STYLE

First the quilting pattern was drawn on paper and then transferred to the quilt top, either by tracing or by using stencils, which might be made from paper or metal. Next, the quilt was placed in a frame for quilting, which involved first placing the backing fabric on the frame, then the wadding, and finally the quilt top. It was then rolled onto the two wooden runners at the top and bottom and secured by tapes to stretchers at each side. As each section was quilted, it was rolled round the far runner to expose the next section to be worked on.

ABOVE Roman sateen quilt in pink and green, made in the north of England c.1900. The very even, precise quilting appears almost Welsh in style, but the patterns used are characteristic of North Country quilts.

RIGHT This superb example of a wholecloth quilt was designed and marked, probably professionally, between 1924 and 1926, but was quilted and finished by Lilian Hedley, of Chester-le-Street in Co. Durham, in 1988. The bordered quilting design was marked by the quilt designer with "Sunflower", "Flat Iron", "Sycamore Leaf", "Shell", and "Leaf" motifs, with some freehand motifs. A square diamond filler has been used.

WHOLECLOTH QUILTS

"His quilts with country fame were crowned." A. Wright, from a poem on the murder of "Joe the Quilter"

Wholecloth quilts from the north-east of England are often referred to as "Durham" or "Northumberland" quilts, which is where the finest examples were made. The marking of the designs on large quilt tops required considerable skill and experience, and quilts were marked

and made professionally as well as domestically. Elizabeth Sanderson (d. 1934) was both quilter and professional designer and marker. She used a blue pencil for marking quilt tops and could complete two in a day. She also established her own workshop to design and mark out quilt tops, and took in apprentices to teach them the traditional skills. Another legendary figure in the quilting

LEFT Plain gold quilt, 1939. The gold sateen on both sides is very finely quilted, with a central rose enclosed within a circle and an elaborate design of leaves, flowers, and feathers radiating from the centre. It was made by Mrs Mary Potts, a widow who made her living by quilting.

ABOVE "Club" quilt, 1890, in white sateen on both sides with a border of printed floral cotton. It was made by Sally Ranson, a widow who raised her family by running a quilting club. These clubs were run in the mining villages by women whose husbands had been killed or injured in pit accidents. Customers paid a small weekly sum, usually one shilling, until the full cost of the quilt was paid.

history of England's north-east was Joe Hedley, known locally as "Joe the Quilter". He had trained originally as a tailor, but acquired a repuation as a fine professional quilter. Tragically, in 1826, aged 76, he was murdered by persons unknown, who no doubt believed that he had accumulated large sums of money from his quilting. His murder was commemorated by a poet named A. Wright.

STRIPPY QUILTS

The homely strip quilts of northern England, known locally as "strippy" quilts, are made of alternating strips (often fabric strips left over from other quilts) seamed together lengthwise. The earliest strippy so far recorded was made on the Isle of Man around 1840, and is pieced in strips of crimson and black wool. However, most surviving strippies were produced between 1860 and 1930 in Northumberland and Durham, where they were made in great numbers. The quilting patterns were usually arranged in rows down the length of the quilt, the pattern following the strips; in many cases the strips were marked out and quilted one at a time in the frame and joined later. An odd number of strips was usually used so that one strip could be central. The quilting patterns used would be those most appropriate for border patterns, such as twists, plaits, cables, feather twists, and running diamonds. Some strip quilts have alternating plain and patchwork strips, but these are less common. Strippy quilts were a popular choice for quilting clubs because they were relatively quick and easy to make. Favourite colours were Turkey red and white, and blue or green with alternating white strips; printed cottons were also used.

LEFT A classic example of a 19th-century strippy quilt, in which the quilting pattern is contained within the boundaries of each strip. By convention, there is almost always an uneven number of strips in a strippy quilt – five, seven, and nine are the most common – no doubt to achieve symmetry in the overall design.

ABOVE Patchwork strip quilt, 1877. A typical "pieced strippy" quilt formed from six strips of printed fabric and five strips composed of pieced squares on a salmon-pink background. The quilting follows the strips in twist and running diamond patterns. Finely made with a piped edge, the quilt is dated 1877 and signed "J. Foster".

"Undercover Angels" by Sheena Norquay, 1999. Wholecloth quilted wall hanging made of cotton sateen and muslin with a wool batting, using free machine-quilting and some embroidery, trapunto, and satin stitching. This is a contemporary interpretation of the wholecloth tradition, inspired by Italian sculpture seen in the British Museum and by decoration on furniture reproduced in a book on historical ornament.

"Rivers VII" by Helen Parrott, 1995. A wholecloth quilted wall hanging made of hand-dyed fabrics and applied threads, hand- and machine-quilted. The artist has re-interpreted the wholecloth tradition to produce a sculptural, fluid piece of art that is wholly contemporary, and far removed from its more functional historical antecedents. The quilted pattern ripples across the surface, creating an abstract effect of a riverbed.

SCOTLAND : HISTORY AND TRADITIONS

The few quilts that have survived in Scotland from before the 19th century suggest that quilting was mainly confined to work commissioned by the wealthy. As in other parts of Great Britain, quilting during the 17th and much of the 18th century was part of the embroiderer's repertoire, to fulfil the requirements of aristocrats and other wealthy families for luxurious domestic items such as bed coverings, bed curtains, and pillows. An exhibition of art needlework held in Edinburgh in 1877 featured some notable survivals, including an embroidered quilt said to date from the 17th century and to have covered the bed of an archbishop. Another exhibition in 1934, by the Scottish Women's Rural Institute, contained a quilted skirt in red satin that had been worn by a noblewoman in 1745 and, later, by her great-grand-daughter at an Assembly held by Queen Victoria in Edinburgh. Sadly, neither of these items has survived today, but they serve to illustrate the level of society that would have had access to such luxurious items.

EARLY TRADITIONAL QUILTS

Although patchwork coverlets were made in the 19th century in much of Scotland, there is little evidence of actual quilts being made until toward the middle of the 19th century. One of the earliest recorded traditional-style quilts is a wholecloth made in Fifeshire around 1860 by a blacksmith's wife, while a remarkable patchwork quilt was made by Nicholas White of Dundee, who was a whaling ship steward; it is a striking medallion quilt of red and white printed cottons, using fabrics from a book of cotton samples, roughly quilted in an all-over wave pattern.

That so few early traditional quilts have survived suggests that quiltmaking was not widespread in Scotland. No doubt the particular social and economic conditions contributed to this situation; many people lived in conditions of austerity, and in a wool-producing country woollen blankets would probably have been relatively cheap. Any quilts that were made were likely to have incorporated already well-worn materials and to have been washed and used to the point of disintegration.

QUILTING IN THE LATE-19TH CENTURY

In the latter part of the 19th century quiltmaking became more widespread, particularly in the Border regions, where those quilts that have survived, understandably, show strong links with the patterns and traditions of the

RIGHT Turkey red and white "Log Cabin" quilt, made around 1870. Scotland, Ireland, and the Isle of Man are all traditional strongholds of the "Log Cabin" quilt tradition. Turkey red printed fabrics feature frequently in Scottish "Log Cabin" quilts, and indeed in other traditional quilts from around the middle of the 19th century and onward into the 20th, largely because of the fact that Glasgow had been the most important centre in Britain for the production of Turkey red cloth since the late 18th century.

LEFT Linen quilt, early 18th century. Detail showing the centre of the quilt, which is beautifully embellished with crewel embroidery. The quilting is very fine and elaborate. This is an example of the sort of work that would have been commissioned by more affluent people. It is often thought that quilts of this type were embroidered after the background quilting was completed, but that is not always true; this example was quilted from the back and the quilting stitches go through the crewelwork flowers.

neighbouring English North Country quilts. Purely utilitarian quilts were still being made within living memory in these Border regions. In the course of research carried out during the early 1980s, Dorothy Osler recorded the memories of women in Eyemouth, a fishing village on the east coast of the Scottish Borders, who worked as herring-gutters at the beginning of the 20th century.

They made functional, blanket-filled quilts, but only in the winter time because "… i' the summertime ye worked fra six o'clock in the morning ti' twelve a' night guttin' fish". As in the north of England, professional quilters worked in the Borders villages, working to commission and sometimes making quilts for villagers to give as wedding presents for family and friends.

INLAY PATCHWORK

Inlay patchwork, in which small pieces of cloth are inserted into a background and then stitched into place, is a technique that can be compared to the craft of marquetry. It was produced in Britain during the last part of the 19th century, apparently almost exclusively by tailors, who would have had available to them the sort of heavy, non-fraying uniform or suit cloth from which it was made. It demanded a high degree of skill and patience, and so was a very exacting form of patchwork that was used to create wonderful pictures that might otherwise only have been made by appliqué or embroidery techniques.

Some of the most outstanding examples are Scottish, including the famous "Royal Clothograph Work of Art". This took 18 years to finish, and after the death of its maker in 1888 it was raffled on behalf of his widow. It is made of uniform materials, and the number of pieces in each of its seven pictures is recorded meticulously in embroidery. Among other surviving examples are two wall hangings by David Robertson of Falkirk. One features a ship in a central panel surrounded by pictures of various figures including cavalrymen, archers, and a pierrot; it measures 259 x 272cm (102 x 186in) and took 1,650 hours to make!

LEFT The "Royal Clothograph Work of Art", made by John Monro of Paisley, an artist and tailor who was born in 1811. The individual scenes are framed by bands of triangles, and the whole is surrounded by a border embroidered with the names of various notables and intellectuals, along with pious and uplifting sentiments enjoining such virtues as piety, patience, perseverance, and punctuality. It ends: "Love God and Man, Amen".

SOLDIERS' QUILTS

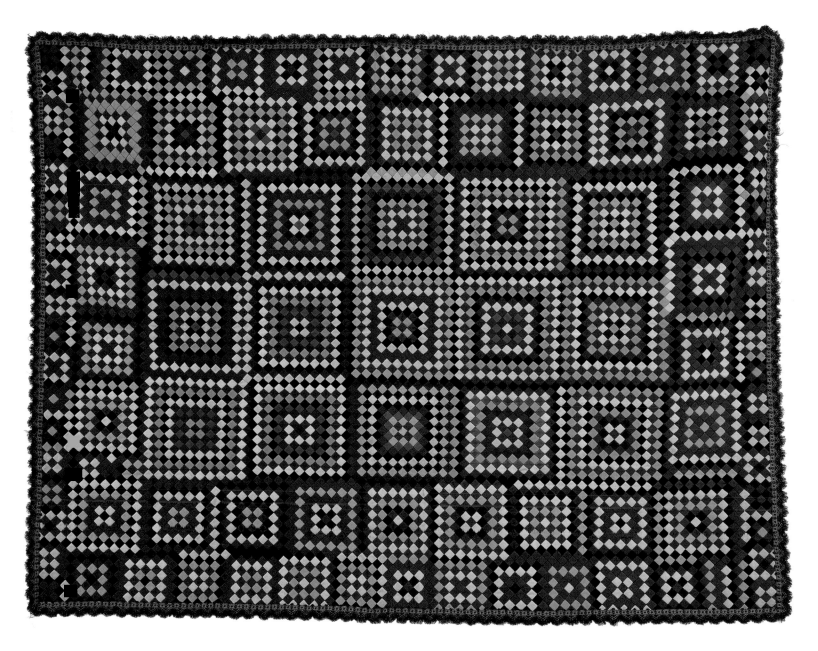

There are many surviving examples of patchwork made by men, usually soldiers, during the late 1800s. They are almost invariably pieced from regular geometric shapes and feature hundreds of tiny pieces of uniform fabric, which at the time were very colourful, resulting in wonderfully vibrant and complex quilts. Sewing patchwork was a good way not only of filling in time when soldiers were not on active service, but also of producing warm coverings. The soldiers vied to incorporate as many pieces of cloth as possible; one patchwork table cover was said to contain 15,500 pieces of cloth in 15 different colours!

Soldiers' quilts are, of course, very heavy because of the cloth used, making sewing right through the material impossible, but some of them were lined and decorated with fringed borders. Some particularly outstanding examples of soldiers' quilts were made by Scottish soldiers, including the one illustrated here that dates from about 1880. It was made by Colour Sergeant R. Cumming of the Highland Light Infantry and was exhibited in the Royal Military Exhibition of 1890 at the Royal Hospital in Chelsea, in aid of the Church of England Soldiers' Institutes.

ABOVE Patchwork quilt, c.1880, made by Colour Sergeant R. Cumming while stationed at Maryhill Barracks in Glasgow. It is pieced entirely from 2.5cm (1in) squares cut from uniform cloth of the Highland Light Infantry, and is backed with printed cotton and edged with a fringe. The maker showed great artistry in the choice and placement of colour to create a brilliant graphic effect, reminiscent of the colours and shapes seen in some Indian *rallis* (see pages 42–3).

"Feathers Collection", by Pauline Burbidge, Berwickshire, 2003. The artist lives in the Scottish Borders, and uses the natural environment as inspiration for her work. This piece, made from collaged and painted cotton and silk fabrics with feathers, is one of a series of quilts incorporating objects collected from around her home – in this case, feathers from swans, crows, and pigeons. The intention is to encourage us to look harder and more appreciatively at the natural beauty around us.

"Angelica gigas", **Angela Chisholm, Edinburgh, 2002.** This dramatic form of angelica caught the eye of the artist, who is herself a keen plantswoman, in the Royal Botanic Gardens, Edinburgh. The image was painted onto silk organza, which was layered over pieces of coloured silk and then machine-embroidered and quilted.

WALES : HISTORY AND TRADITIONS

"Almost every household kept aside at least one 'special' quilt for important occasions, such as a visit from a faraway relative, or... the local doctor." Jen Jones, *Welsh Quilts*

Quilting in Wales can be traced back to the 16th century, but until the 18th century, as elsewhere in Europe, decorative quilts appeared mainly in the homes of the affluent. They often consisted of patchwork in early chintzes with exceptionally fine needlework and elaborate quilting patterns, perhaps made by the young women of well-to-do families as part of the sewing skills that they were encouraged to acquire in preparation for marriage.

QUILTING IN THE COMMUNITY

Quilted bed covers were mainly utilitarian items, often pieces of heavy woollen fabric encasing an old blanket. Until well into the 19th century commercially produced fabrics were expensive, and so the impoverished relied on homespun woollen blankets, used either singly or quilted roughly together. The high period of Welsh quilting dates from around 1840, when less expensive roller-printed fabrics became more easily available. Quiltmaking became widespread, especially in some of the rural counties, where in farmhouses and cottages women quilted not only for themselves but also often to earn a living.

During the 19th century regional differences in style between Welsh quilts and those made in other parts of Britain began to appear. As in Ireland, quilting in rural areas continued and developed very much removed from outside influence until the middle of the century, when many families emigrated to the USA and began to send back examples of American patchwork and quilting. There are examples of such quilts in the Welsh Folk Museum, including one made by a Mrs Strong of Pittsburgh in about 1870. However, the majority of Welsh quilts continued to replicate the 18th-century style of a central medallion surrounded by borders. All types of quilts were popular: patchwork, wholecloth, and, to a lesser degree, appliqué.

Although there was no tradition of communal quilt-making or "sewing bees" as such, home quilters often quilted together as families, and neighbours might work together to make a quilt for each household in turn. Some mothers took pride in making at least one quilt for each son and daughter before they married, and every girl was expected to have stockpiled at least six quilts before her wedding, since they were considered essential items for setting up home. Importantly, quilting developed into a thriving craft industry that enabled many women to earn a living who would otherwise have struggled to survive. As was the case in the north-east of England, many miners' widows supported their families in this way.

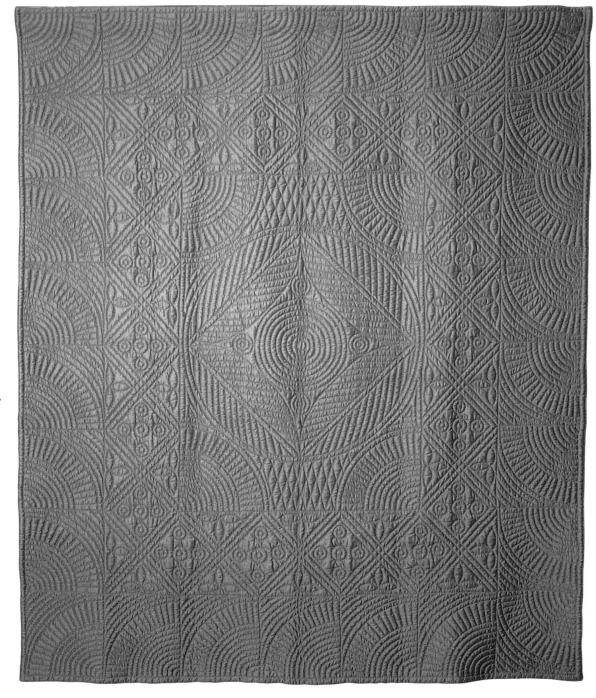

RIGHT Detail of a pink cotton sateen quilt made in Cardiganshire, 1933. The design, with a central motif set in a series of borders, and each border separated by a row of quilting lines, is characteristic of a Welsh wholecloth quilt. The whole central motif is set within a rectangle with fans in the corners, in turn surrounded by two borders quilted with a variety of patterns. The quilt is filled with lambswool, which is very soft and so facilitates the fine quilting stitches.

LEFT Star quilt made by Sarah Lewis of Aberdare. Some of the most spectacular Welsh patchwork quilts are those made from flannels of solid colour, which, when filled with fleece and stitched elaborately with heart, leaf, flower, and diamond motifs, could look extremely elegant. The likeness to Amish quilts is unmistakable.

It was around the mid-19th century that there was an increase in the production of Welsh flannel, resulting in the geometric quilts in strong, saturated colours that have become such a distinctive feature of the Welsh tradition. The designs and colours of these quilts bear such a striking resemblance to those produced by the Amish in parts of the USA, particularly in Pennsylvania (*see* pages 140–3), that it is tempting to surmise that the influx of Welsh settlers had an influence on the Amish style. However, verifiable links between the two styles have yet to be established.

DECLINE OF QUILTING IN WALES

By the end of the 19th century the ready availability of other, cheaper types of bedding, changes in fashion, and poor financial returns for such labour-intensive work led to the decline of quilting. Efforts were made to preserve and revive the traditional skills, notably through schemes designed to provide income in mining regions where the Depression led to extensive unemployment. These operated into the 1930s, but the advent of World War II finally spelt the end of quiltmaking as a craft industry.

PIECED QUILTS

Many Welsh patchwork quilts of the early 19th century were essentially utilitarian and could best be described as "scrap" quilts, no doubt using fabric recycled from other projects. Despite this, many of them show a high standard of design and execution in the quilting. One type of patchwork made during the first half of the 19th century incorporated pieces of woollen fabric from military uniforms, often made by wounded soldiers or sailors as a form of occupational therapy, or by tailors who had scraps of material left over from making uniforms. By far the most popular style for quilts in the first part of the 19th century was a medallion surrounded by a series of borders, sometimes called "frame quilts", and very similar in style to the most characteristic examples of English quilting made at that time. Patchwork quilts became far more common after the 1830s, when the development of roller printing resulted in the availability, at a reasonable price, of mass-produced printed cottons. There are more examples of appliqué quilts and patterns toward the end of the century, such as "Log Cabin" and "Flying Geese" – patterns familiar in American quilts and probably, in many cases, acquired from relatives in America.

LEFT Chintz patchwork, c.1840, Swansea. Patchworks containing chintz were relatively rare in Wales, and usually put together from recycled fabrics. This frame design was one of the most frequently used styles during the 19th century.

WHOLECLOTH QUILTS

Welsh quilts incorporate many different patterns, but the overall design on the vast majority of quilts of all periods features a centre medallion surrounded by a series of borders. Within that general framework there was scope for individual quilters to make their own variations, so that no two quilts are identical. Patterns might be passed on from mother to daughter, or from professional quilter to apprentice. The most common filling for quilts was wool, but both cotton and wool were used for the top; the finest stitching is usually found on the cotton varieties since they were easier to quilt. From the mid-19th century onward cotton and cotton sateen became the most popular fabrics. Cotton sateen is a wonderfully soft cotton with a slight sheen, which was widely available in solid colours, prints, and florals. The plain version highlights the quilting patterns to perfection, so that was used most frequently for wholecloth quilts. However, quite often a quilt top would be floral and the back a solid colour; some said that the floral side was for "every day", since it would be less likely to show any dirt or wear, whereas the plain side, displaying the full beauty of the quilting pattern, would be reserved for "best".

WHOLECLOTH QUILTS: METHOD AND STYLE

Almost without exception, Welsh quilts were made on a frame. The most common fillings were old blankets and lambswool, although professional quiltmakers might purchase cotton wadding. Motifs were traced onto the fabric prior to quilting, usually with tailor's chalk, and any household items that were readily to hand were used to draw the pattern: plates, glasses, and cups might be pressed into service. Templates and stencils made from pieces of cardboard were also used and, occasionally, purpose-made metal templates; edges, corners, and straight lines were drawn with rulers. Very experienced quilters might chalk the designs freehand.

LEFT Although Welsh quilting patterns vary from region to region, quilts made in Wales can easily be distinguished from English North Country quilts, or indeed from European or American pieces. The designs are generally more geometric than those found on North Country quilts, and draw on a particular repertoire of motifs. A typical Welsh quilt has a large medallion in the centre, surrounded by a series of quilted borders, each of which is delineated by one or two rows of stitching.

RIGHT Detail of a wholecloth quilt showing both the top and the reverse of the exquisite quilting stitches. The quilt was made by Miss Emiah Jones for a quilting competition held at the Welsh Folk Museum, St Fagans, Cardiff, in 1951.

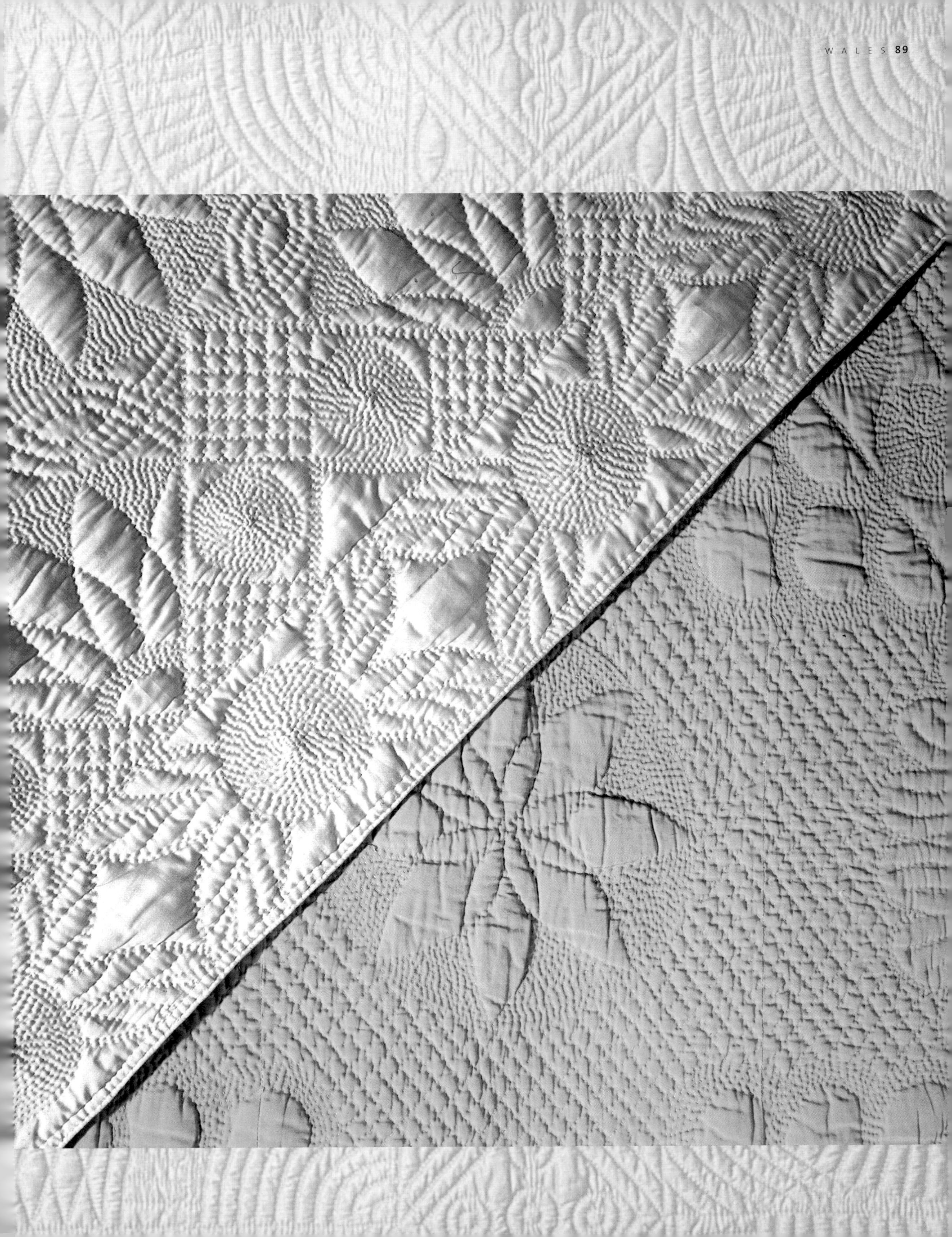

"Patterns of the Past", by Barbara Howell, 1991. This original design based on traditional quilting patterns uses free machine-quilting and embroidery and was first exhibited at the Welsh National Eisteddfod at Mold in 1991, where it was the winner in its class. This is one of Barbara Howell's earliest quilts, and it incorporates Elizabethan motifs as well as the hearts that are representative of traditional Welsh quilting patterns.

"Ringing the Changes", by Gwenfai Rees Griffiths, 1998. The artist says that she is a traditionalist at heart, and many of her quilts reflect her Welsh roots. However, in this piece she has interpreted an American block pattern, "Double Wedding Ring", in an original way. Machine-pieced, hand-appliquéd, and quilted, inside each of the 20 shaded rings there are 10 different distorted nine-patch blocks, while hand-appliqué dog roses ramble through the rings.

IRELAND : HISTORY AND TRADITIONS

Decorative patchwork and quilting appear to have been introduced to Ireland during the 18th century, when English ladies living on their large country estates taught needlework skills, including patchwork and quilting, to their servants. They in turn passed the crafts to surrounding cottages, villages, and towns, where the growth and popularity of patchwork and quilting no doubt rested on the usual combination of thrift, necessity, and pleasure in pattern-making. Most traditional Irish patchwork quilts consist of only two layers, quilted together with a wave,

or chevron, pattern. This is also the pattern most often seen on quilts from the north-west coast of England, underlining the strong cultural ties linking these two adjacent regions.

UTILITARIAN QUILTS

Solid, utilitarian quilts were made in the colder and more mountainous areas of Ireland, where it was usual to stitch together layers of worn blankets and cover them in a rough patchwork of hand-woven fabrics, tweeds, and old suit materials. The patchwork was often pieced in

LEFT Pieced and appliquéd bed quilt of plain and printed cottons, c.1870, believed to have been made by a member of the Knox family of County Antrim. The central appliquéd motif is formed from a single piece of fabric that has been folded and cut into a pattern known throughout Northern Ireland as either "Heart and Spade" or "Heart and Dove" – a pattern that was especially popular for wedding quilts. The quilt is hand-quilted in the "wave" pattern, the most common pattern found not only along the east coast of Ireland but also in south-west Scotland and on the west coast of Cumbria, providing some evidence of cultural exchange between these neighbouring regions.

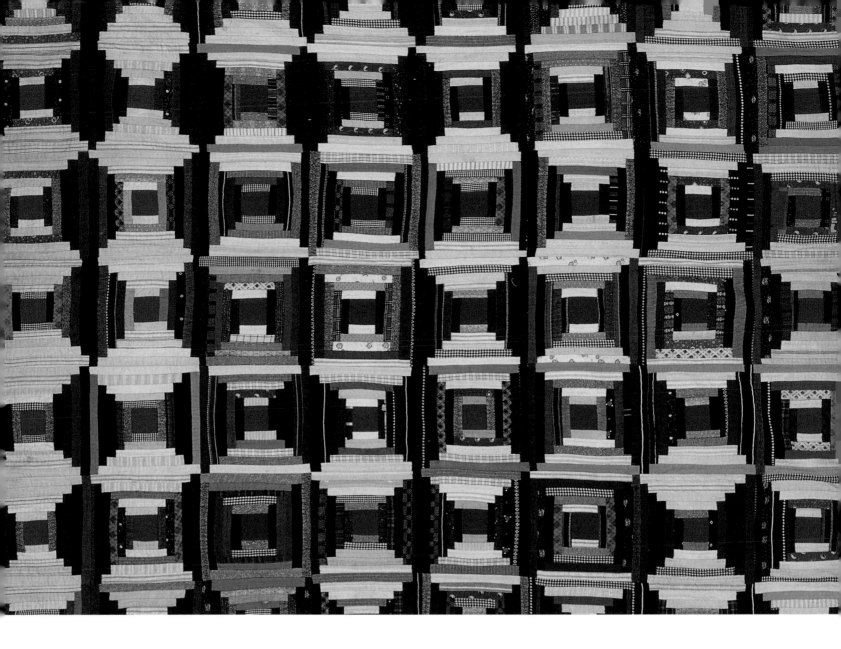

ABOVE "Log Cabin" bed quilt, hand-pieced in wool and cotton strips. It was made in about 1900 by Jane Bleakney of County Armagh. The Ulster Folk and Transport Museum in Northern Ireland has the largest quilt collection in the British Isles, containing about 500 items altogether. Around 40 of them are "Log Cabin" quilts, including some examples of unusual variations on the "Log Cabin" theme. This one is the only example in the collection of what is known in the USA as the "Courthouse Steps" version of the pattern.

"Log Cabin" blocks (also a common pattern in the Isle of Man, where many Irish farming families settled). These rough and ready, but serviceable, quilts were usually tied with sheep's wool rather than quilted.

Once sewing machines became available, patchworks were often hand-pieced and then machine-quilted. However, very few people owned their own machine, so machine-quilting was proudly displayed, even if the quilts had been taken to the local dressmaker's or clothes factory to be quilted!

PATCHWORK QUILTS

In the north of Ireland, Turkey red and white patchwork quilts featured strongly, and were often referred to as "best quilts", kept for special occasions such as a visit from the doctor. If any home lacked such a quilt, neighbours would rally round and lend one when needed. Many women kept rag-bags for patchwork: any unneeded or

worn-out fabrics were recycled, along with shop samples, and scraps acquired from dressmakers, travellers, and factories. A number of shirt factories gave offcuts to their workers, and as a consequence some patchworks comprise a wonderful selection of striped fabrics.

IRISH TRADITION

It has been remarked that the Irish quilt shows a distinct lack of development in both style and technique from its early versions. This may be explained by the fact that the Irish lived in villages and small communities where there was widespread poverty and little opportunity to travel, short of emigrating. Quilting traditions were simply passed down from one generation to the next, little affected by outside influence until large numbers of Irish started emigrating to America. Over the years the Irish-American connection was kept alive by the exchange of patchwork and quilting patterns between the two nations.

TRADITIONAL QUILTS

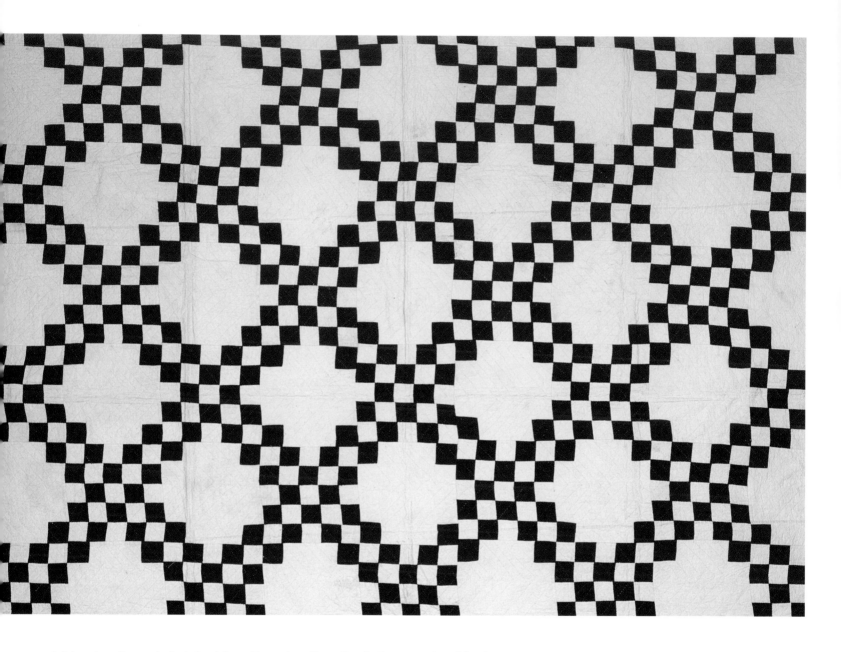

Patchwork quilts made in Ireland from the early 19th century onward appear with all the patterns found in English quilts, including the familiar hexagons in all-over quilts, crazy quilts, strip quilts, and, of course, "Log Cabin". In many of the quilts surviving from this period there is a strong American influence evident in both the patterns and styles. The "Irish Chain" pattern, for example, was known in America from early in the 19th century, but we cannot be certain whether it had earlier Irish connections. Nevertheless, it certainly became a popular pattern in Ireland.

Two further examples of familiar American blocks found in Irish quilts are "Drunkard's Path" (*see* page 139) and "Orange Peel". This American connection is illustrated by the discovery in Northern Ireland of a quilt that is backed with flour bags from Ohio, although there is no record of when or how they got to Ireland! However, the damask linen and the dye used for the top fabrics confirm that the quilt is indeed Irish. Appliqué quilts also appear to have been very popular, particularly those using Turkey red fabric motifs on a white background.

LEFT "Irish Chain" patchwork quilt, hand-pieced in Turkey red and white cotton, with a white cotton backing. It was made by Agnes Annie Smith of County Antrim as a wedding quilt for her marriage in 1891. "Irish Chain" is one of the oldest quilt-pattern names in the USA. However, the earliest example is derived from a weaving pattern that it resembles, rather than any specifically Irish connection.

BELOW Bed quilt of Turkey red cotton motifs created by the "fold and cut" method and appliquéd to a white cotton background. The central motif is a stylized version of the "Heart and Dove" so popular in Northern Ireland. Probably late-19th century, it is entirely machine-quilted in a diamond pattern. The use of red appliqué on a white background is a distinctive feature of Irish quilting.

"Ligoniel. An Irish Linen Village" by Roselind Shaw, 1993, records the history of a now-defunct linen village in Northern Ireland, where the maker's grandfather went to work at Wolfhill Spinning Mill when he was 13 years old. The story of the village is told on 48 hand-embroidered linen squares, which are divided by strips of petersham ribbon, and the quilt is tied with linen buttons. The last square reads: "This quilt was wrought by Roselind Shaw née McClintock in memory of her Grandfather Samuel McClintock 1878–1962 and her father Victor McClintock 1908–91, who were both on the staff at Wolfhill Spinning Mill. Completed Nov 1993."

"Wall Arrangement" by Bryde Glynn, 1987. The Burren is an area on the west coast of Ireland famous for its outstandingly beautiful natural scenery and flora, as well as its wonderful stone walls. This quilt, made from Irish tweeds and wool, pieced and applied to a cotton and tweed background, was made as a result of a Crafts Council of Ireland project, for which 22 artists, working in various media, spent a week on the Burren.

FRANCE : HISTORY AND TRADITIONS

"The bed at Cuchous and its singular furnishings opened to me the doors of an unknown universe..." Janine Jannière, "An Important Discovery of French Patchwork", *Antiques Magazine*

The region of France that is most famous for its quilting traditions is Provence, and the terms "Marseilles quilts" and *boutis* are familiar to many quiltmakers. Indeed, the fame of Provençal quilts has tended to obscure the fact that quilting was practised in many parts of France. To make matters worse, there is very little documentation of the French tradition in general, but some notable examples of quilting, such as luxurious bed furnishings found in provincial châteaux, bear testimony to its widespread use from at least the 17th century. Beautifully executed mosaic-style patchwork quilts, some of them made by ordinary village women, also survive from the early 19th century.

From early in the 17th century the brilliantly coloured cottons known as *indiennes* were being imported from India, and examples of the many quilts and other articles that were made from these highly desirable fabrics still survive. Clearly, quilting was a thriving and widespread tradition, although much of the elaborate and labour-intensive work commissioned for the homes of the wealthy would have been carried out in ateliers (studios). An outstanding example of the needlework skills of the 17th-century quilters is triumphantly displayed in a set of sumptuous gold silk bed furnishings at the Château de Grignan, which provides evidence of the luxurious articles that the wealthy could afford to commission.

As for patchwork, any suggestion that it was necessarily associated with poverty can be discounted by a remarkable set of patchwork bed furnishings that came to the attention of the French quilt scholar, Janine Jannière, in 1990. The bed furnishings, dating from between 1820 and 1830, were found at the Château de Cuchous, Pyrénées-Orientales, and comprised a bed cover, two curtains, and two festooned canopies, all elaborately pieced over papers in what has become known as the English patchwork style (*see* page 58). It is an outstanding example of mosaic patchwork, with the pattern built up from hexagons to form rosettes. Even more remarkable is the fact that at regular intervals the toiles have been cut in such a way as to create pictures, each one covering the surface of one, seven, or 37 hexagons, and it has been possible to identify the exact figurative toiles used in this way, most of them being *Toiles de Jouy* (the famous printed fabrics produced at Jouy-en-Josas).

Inspired by the discovery, Jannière has carried out research into the use of mosaic patchwork in France and has uncovered, as she has put it, an "unknown universe". As a result, evidence of the popularity of mosaic patch-work, and particularly of the use of hexagons, has been identified in other, previously undocumented, examples, mainly from the third quarter of the 18th century.

LEFT Detail of quilted petticoat dating from the end of the 18th century, made from Indian chintz. The quilting on such articles tended to be quite plain, since the main decorative effect was achieved in the fabric itself. Quilting patterns were simple grids of squares or diamonds, and the standard finish for borders, as on this petticoat, was one or more rows of cording run through narrowly stitched channels.

ABOVE Bed furnishings in gold silk, in the Count's bedchamber at the Château de Grignan, near Orange. These are the height of elegant style and luxury. They exemplify the exquisite, but very labour-intensive, workmanship that the wealthy could afford to commission from the ateliers that specialized in this sort of needlework.

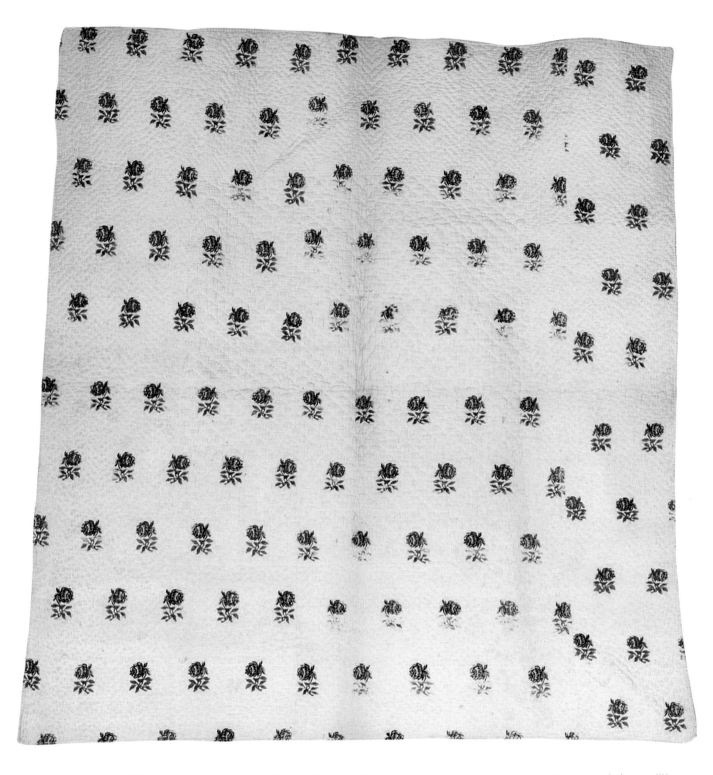

LEFT Two bed curtains, which form part of the pieced mosaic bed furnishings at the Château de Cuchous, an isolated château that has been occupied by the same family since 1700. They incorporate particular *Toile de Jouy* fabrics that have been identified as "La Noce de Campagne", "Tancrède", "La Chasse à Jouy", and "Le Vampire". Altogether no fewer than 33 figurative toiles (19 from Jouy) have been identified in the entire set of furnishings.

ABOVE French provincial coverlet in ivory silk dating from the late 18th century. The coverlet is embroidered with stylized rose sprigs in blue, red, and green wools to simulate silk brocade. Although the coverlet itself is from around the end of the 18th century, the quilting, which is in a cross-hatched diamond pattern, was added only in the 19th century.

As elsewhere in Europe, needlework, including quilting, embroidery, and appliqué, was regarded as a suitable occupation for aristocratic young ladies. Records of the French Revolution make reference to a wedding quilt made for Marie Antoinette, the young queen, by the ladies of her mother's court, which took eight years to make. Elaborately appliquéd with flowers, cupids, and other symbols of love, it was cited by her accusers as another example of her excessive extravagance!

QUILTED CLOTHES

Throughout much of the 17th and 18th centuries many types of garment were quilted. In France a large number of dresses, caps, and jackets survive, while others can be seen depicted in the paintings of the time. Antoine Raspal (1738–1811) illustrated a sleeping baby swaddled in an outfit quilted in an overall diamond pattern, and produced many portraits of stylish women wearing clothing that displays *broderie de Marseille*, the corded style of quilting from Provence. So popular was this style that it was used for camisoles, corsets, bonnets, and even pockets, which were then separate items tied round the waist underneath skirts. Quilted petticoats remained highly fashionable for a long time: they ranged from elaborately quilted luxurious silk petticoats, often displayed under open-fronted gowns, to more modest cotton versions quilted in simple patterns – usually a diamond grid.

By the end of the 17th century *indiennes* were so much in demand that they were being made into quilted bed covers, throws, wall coverings, gowns, and dressing gowns until, under pressure from the French textile manufacturers, a complete ban was placed on their importation.

BELOW Quilted petticoat dating from the first half of the 19th century. Imitations of highly desirable Indian chintzes were being produced in France from the middle of the 17th century, and in the 19th century the term *indiennes* was applied loosely to all printed cottons, irrespective of where they were produced. The block-printed *indienne* in this petticoat was actually produced by the Oberkampf factory at Jouy-en-Josas around 1807.

LEFT Back view of a ceremonial headdress, c.1840–60. This headdress is believed to come from Rochefort or La Rochelle. The decoration is described as *boutis* (corded quilting), but it reflects the changes in hand-stitched wholecloth whitework during the 19th century because it has batting between the two layers of cloth.

BELOW Woman's long-sleeved bodice dating from around 1790, displaying *boutis* work on white muslin and cotton. Indigo-dyed blue cording has been inserted into the stitched channels to emphasize the pattern. This example is typical of the *boutis* style of quilting made in Arles, and is on display in the Museon Arlaten.

PATCHWORK QUILTS AND COVERLETS

The very sophisticated 19th-century patchwork bed furnishings at the Château de Cuchous speak of a long and continuous tradition of expertise in patchwork that was clearly perpetuated both in the ateliers and in rural areas, where women made patchwork for themselves and their families. Janine Jannière found a significant number of patchwork quilts in the mosaic style, often featuring the familiar hexagon shape. An interesting exception to the hexagon mosaic is a silk patchwork quilt pieced from triangles by Honorine Gibault, a hatmaker from a village in the Yonne region. But mosaic patchwork was certainly not the only style employed, as the remarkable works of Marie Beurthonelle, born in 1862 in a village in the Deux-Sèvres region, prove. She won local fame with her artistic "assemblages" of small scraps of leftover fabrics, which she acquired from dressmakers and tailors. Her quilts are true works of art, created by a simple countrywoman without artistic training of any sort but with an innate aesthetic sense. It seems that more research and documentation is needed before any general conclusions can be reached about the use of pattern and style in early French patchwork.

LEFT Quilted coverlet, probably a wedding quilt, made in the first half of the 19th century but pieced from Indian chintz fabrics dating from the end of the 18th century. The centre field of this remarkable patchwork features a central medallion surrounded by a series of borders. The whole quilt is bordered by a pale green silk – apparently recycled Chinese silk, or *pekinee* – embroidered with red and green flowers. The use of green on wedding quilts is symbolic of fertility and renewal.

ABOVE Silk mosaic patchwork, third quarter
of the 19th century, made by Honorine
Gibault, a hatmaker of Quarre-les-Tombes
in the Yonne district who was born in 1837
and lived to be a hundred. She achieved
local fame for her quilts, and her village
honoured her with a gift of a silver box.

QUILTING TRADITIONS OF PROVENCE

"What distinguished the work of Provençal needlewomen was their vision of the decorative possibilities inherent in these lines and stitches." Kathryn Berensen, *Quilts of Provence*

While Provençal quilts made from the famous *indiennes* reflect the glorious natural colours of that region, it is the all-white, wholecloth, corded, and hand-quilted Marseilles needlework that is the great glory of the French tradition. Stretching back seven centuries, Marseilles needlework was continued by skilled needlewomen in fishing villages along the Mediterranean coast until World War I. The exquisite hand-stitching (*broderie de Marseille*) was used to create elaborate designs with intertwined floral forms, vines, garlands, and many other motifs. Worked on two layers of fabric, it involved introducing fine cording through stitched lines following a pattern drawn onto the top cloth. From the 17th to the mid-18th century the finest examples were probably made in ateliers. In 1763 a patent was obtained in England for a method of producing machine-made cloth simulating the hand-stitched work. This was so successful that by 1800, certainly in America, Marseilles quilting suggested machine-made work.

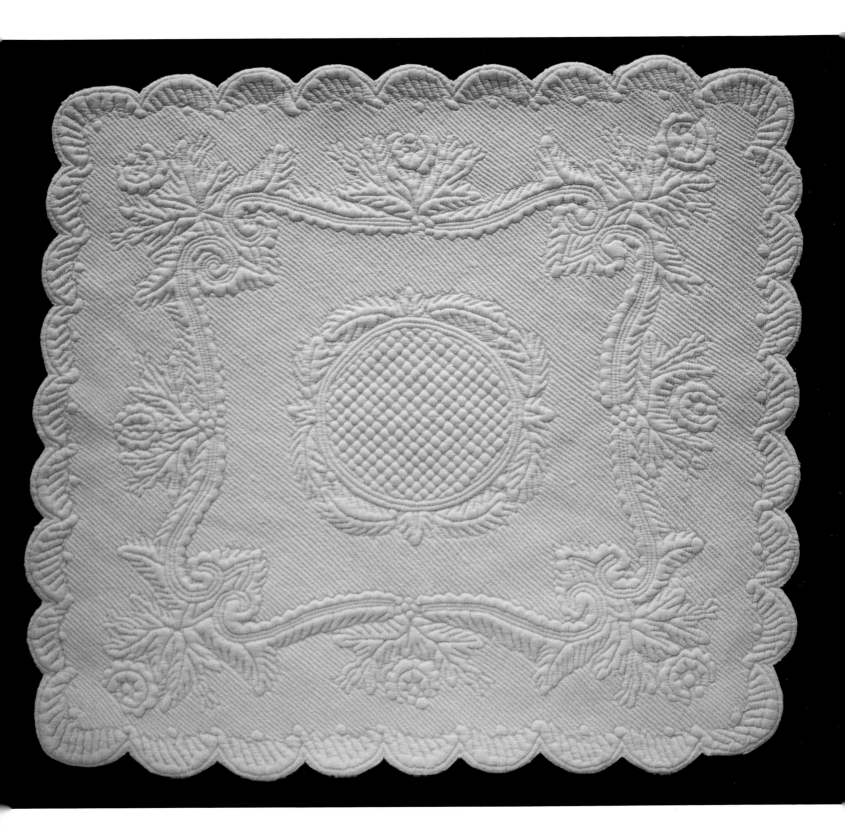

LEFT Detail of an exquisitely quilted silk *vanne* (small quilted bed cover) from Provence, displaying characteristically vivid Provençal colours. Quilted articles of silk, originally imported from China, India, and Italy but later produced in France, were luxury items.

ABOVE *Petassouns* were small lap quilts designed to cover and protect clothing while babies were fed and changed. The all-white versions, of which this is an example, were intended for christenings and other special occasions, whereas more practical items for everyday use might be made from printed cotton fabrics.

BOUTIS: METHOD AND STYLE

Boutis is a 19th-century Provençal word describing the quilted needlework technique that involves drawing cording through narrow lines of stitching; it also refers to the blunt-nosed needle used in this technique. A template is used to trace a pattern on the top layer of fine white cotton fabric, which is then outlined in parallel lines using tiny running stitches. Cording is drawn through the channels and definition is given to the pattern elements, such as flowers and leaves, by inserting small circles of cording into them from the back.

ABOVE Detail showing the original style of corded quilting, worked on two layers of fabric with small coils of cording thread inserted into the flowers and leaves. Very fine detailing of stylized floral patterns, garlands, and leafy vines characterized this type of work. Later it became usual to insert small pieces of wadding into the pattern shapes in place of cording.

RIGHT Detail of a wedding quilt, c.1800. By the mid-18th century trade restrictions resulted in diminished domestic and foreign markets for Marseilles needlework, which in turn affected production methods. Thereafter, ateliers produced stuffed needlework, in which the surface relief is more exaggerated and sculptural — an effect achieved by inserting pieces of cotton wadding into the back of the motifs and often a layer of wadding between the top and bottom fabrics as well. Such quilts were often used as decorative items to celebrate weddings.

"Jouy" by Marie-Christine Flocard, 1993. A pieced quilt featuring reprints of some of the renowned fabrics produced at the Oberkampf factory at Jouy-en-Josas during the 18th century, known as *Toiles de Jouy*. The factory was founded in 1760, and its unrivalled expertise with copper-plate and copper-roller printing established the reputation of its fabrics, which became popular throughout France and are to be found in many quilts. This contemporary quilt pays homage to the history of textile printing and patchwork in France.

"Sortilège" by Geneviève Attinger, 2000. This has a background of pieced blocks, some appliquéd with free machine-quilting, others made of curved and interwoven strips. The faces are made of appliquéd fabrics in different colour values to produce effects of light and shadow, and the whole surface is embellished with free machine-embroidery. The quilt is an abstract depiction of a French legend about the impossible love between a human girl and a goblin.

THE NETHERLANDS : HISTORY AND TRADITIONS

"Because of the greater popularity of the American quilt, there is a tendency to believe that [native] quilts were unknown in the Netherlands. If, however, we take the trouble to examine the history of the Dutch quilt, we shall find that it is more interesting than might at first be imagined." An Moonen, *Quilts: The Dutch Tradition* The patchwork and quilting traditions of the Netherlands are among the best documented of any in Europe; this is partly because of an exceptional collection of quilts housed at the Netherlands Open-Air Museum in Arnhem, but is also largely due to the work and research of quilt historian An Moonen, who wrote the catalogue for an exhibition of the museum's quilt collection in 1992.

A LONGSTANDING TRADITION

Quilted bed covers were known in the Netherlands as early as the Middle Ages, but until the import of ready-made chintz quilts from India in the early 17th century, quilts seem to have been quite rare. Early descriptions suggest that they were mostly satin wholecloth quilts.

Examples of Dutch patchwork coverlets made during the last 300 years survive in both private collections and museums; most of these come from the area around the former Zuider Zee. Although it has been claimed that Dutch patchwork quilts had their origins in poverty, the sheer number of expensive fabrics contained within them indicates that they were more likely to have been made by, or for, relatively affluent people.

LEFT Detail of a 17th-century silk quilt. Very few quilts are mentioned in household inventories available to us from this time, which suggests that they must have been quite rare and, as in other parts of Europe, probably owned exclusively by royalty and the aristocracy. It is recorded, for example, that in 1632 the bed covers of Prince William comprised a red silk quilt and two Spanish blankets.

RIGHT Detail of a chintz quilt made in India, c.1700–50, padded with cotton wadding and lined with white silk. The quilting pattern, on the white silk reverse of the quilt, bears no relation to the floral pattern on the top of the quilt, making it, in effect, a reversible quilt. Quilts of this type, with the top made from chintz cut from the bolt, are considered inferior to those with a single pattern (such as the "Tree of Life"). Nonetheless, the reverse of this example reveals a magnificently quilted pattern, with a central floral motif surrounded by rosettes, stars, and a floral border.

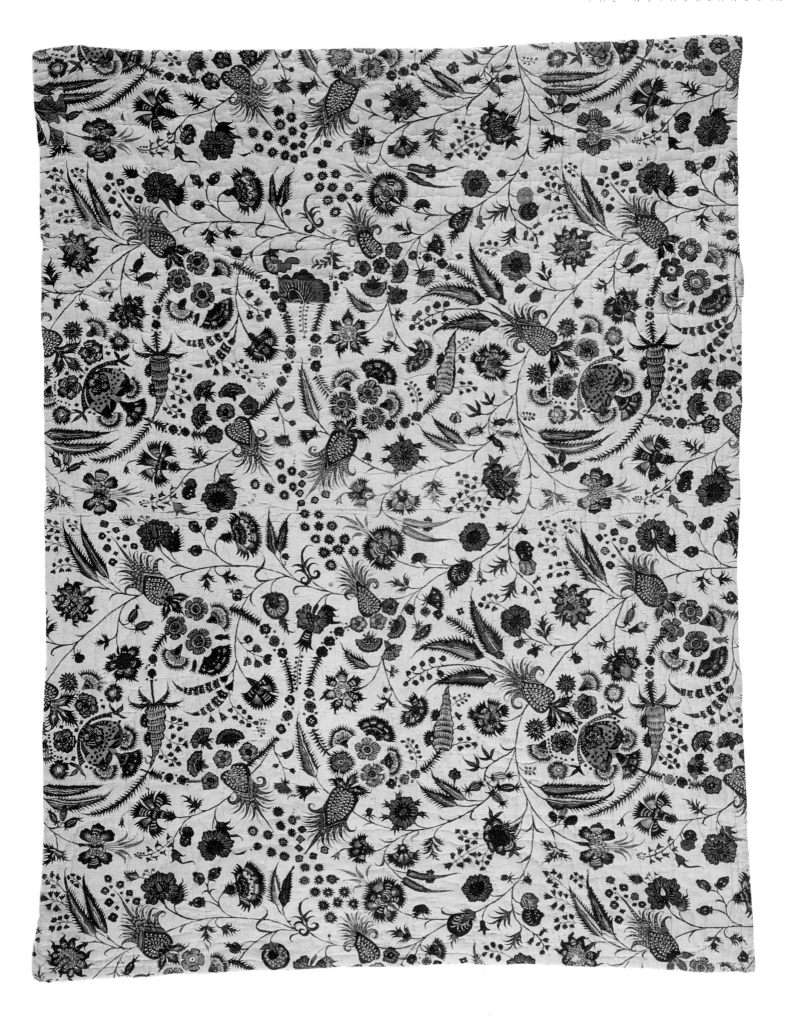

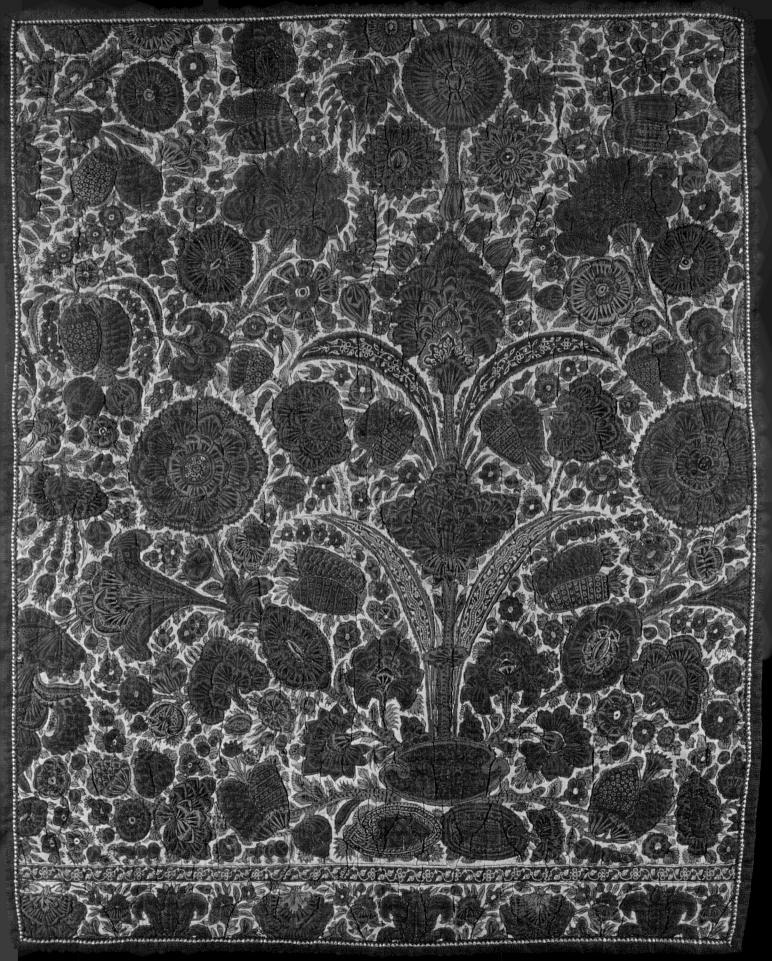

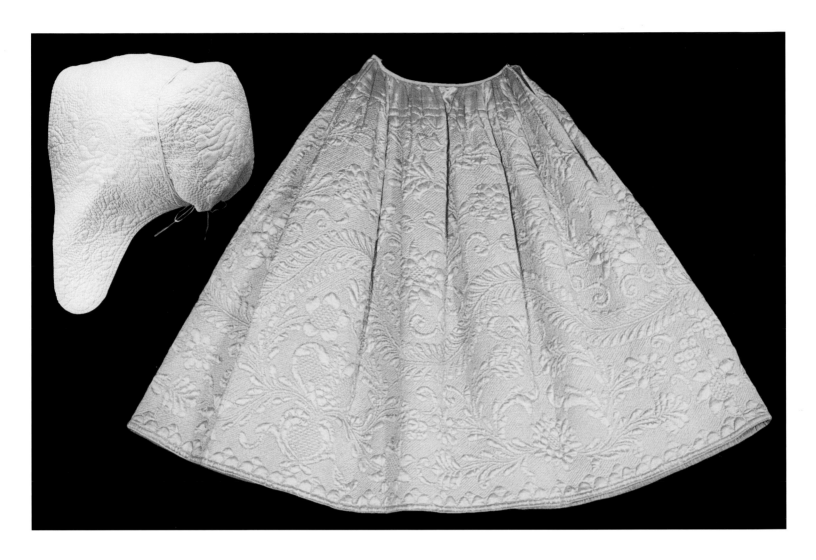

ABOVE Quilting was a distinct craft and was much used on clothing during the 18th century. This woman's cap in the Netherlands Open-Air Museum was made between 1690 and 1700. It is closely quilted with elaborate designs of flowers and infill patterns. The yellow silk petticoat dates from the 18th century and is a particularly splendid quilted version of the style.

LEFT Indian christening quilt, c.1700. A "Tree of Life" motif occupies the whole centrefield, and the quilt is completed with a bottom border of repeated motifs. This is an example of a ready-made, imported quilt bearing a design that was printed specifically for a quilt. The lining is red silk and the quilting follows the pattern on the top. Not all chintz quilts were imported ready-made: chintz was also imported in bulk and sold by the metre to be turned into quilts by local quiltmakers. These quilts tended to be of inferior quality, and often just consisted of a chintz top made from fabric cut from the bolt.

CHINTZ QUILTS

During the 18th century, large numbers of chintz quilts were imported from India by the Dutch East India Company, as records in ships' manifests and order lists show. Many of these quilts have survived, providing evidence of the wonderful variety of patterns and colours, not to mention fine quilting, that made the Indian chintz quilts so desirable in Europe. As the number imported increased with time, these quilts became less exclusive. However, not all surviving examples of chintz quilts were made in India – chintz was also imported by the bolt and purchased by Dutch quiltmakers, some of them working professionally.

QUILTED CLOTHES

Quilted clothing was much used in Holland from at least the 17th century, as in other parts of Europe; paintings by artists such as Vermeer and De Hooch often show people dressed in quilted clothing. In the earliest examples two layers of linen, with a layer of cotton wadding, were made into washable, warm garments. Of course, such everyday garments would have been washed and worn until they were threadbare and fit only to be discarded, so very few have survived.

As quilts became more popular during the 18th century quilted clothing also became more common, but it was made in a different way: the padding was added later, after the quilting was completed. Garments were made from a top layer that might be of linen, cotton, wool, or silk, wadded with wool or cotton, and backed by linen, cotton, or glazed wool. Quilted skirts, quite a few of which can be seen in Dutch museums, became very fashionable and were worn as both over- and underskirts until the end of the 18th century. During the course of the century the quilting patterns on clothing changed from simple, all-over square-diamond patterns to more elaborate, flowing designs of flowers and garlands.

PATCHWORK QUILTS

Patchwork seems to have emerged as a separate technique at the end of the 18th century, probably as a result of the widespread use of chintz and cotton prints for clothing: many families would have had pieces of the then-fashionable chintzes and cotton prints left over from dresses and other household items. Despite the fact that these fabrics were imported into Europe in huge quantities, they would still have been expensive and people would not have wanted to waste them; this would account for the growth of patchwork at this time.

Many decorative uses were found for this technique: in addition to quilts and coverlets, there are surviving examples of scarves and even a cloth to cover a fire basket. It is interesting to note that in the earliest patchworks the shapes used are almost always triangles, and the materials are chintz and cotton prints. As An Moonen observes, the earliest patchwork quilts are like sample books, displaying the range of fabrics in use at the time. Moving into the 19th century, patchwork tended to have what Moonen terms a "typically Dutch look", referring to the triangular shapes and light and dark effects. As the century progressed, hexagons and small squared diamonds became more common, and consequently the appearance of patchwork quilts changed.

LEFT Patchwork coverlet, c.1850. Pieced mainly from plain silk hexagons of about 4cm (1½in) across, this is a brilliant example of the mosaic style. It is not quilted, but lined with cotton print. The pattern has been designed with the utmost care and skill to create a dazzling, and surprisingly modern, effect. The stars recall traditional American patchwork blocks.

ABOVE Detail of a chintz patchwork coverlet, c.1775–1800, pieced from Indian hand-painted chintz, with some European cotton prints – probably French. Dating from the time when chintz was being imported in quantity, it offers a glimpse of the wealth of colours and patterns available. Note the "Dutch look" conferred by the triangles and contrasting light and dark fabrics.

"Queensday on the Island of Marken" by Akka Phillips, 1998. Over the last 50 years it has become the custom on the Island of Marken, off the east coast of Holland, for the colour orange to be worn on 30 April to commemorate the royal House of Orange. This quilt therefore celebrates a part of local Dutch history.

"Interwoven" by Dirke van der Horst-Beetsma. This complex image has been created using a combination of appliqué and embroidery, and incorporates cotton, silk, linen, and polyester fabrics. Small pieces of material have been cut freely, and sewn directly onto the cotton background without the use of pins or glue. This artist works intuitively, inspired mainly by the fabrics that she selects and combines in response to some general design ideas in her head. The quilt develops as she works.

SCANDINAVIA : HISTORY AND TRADITIONS

ABOVE Patchwork quilt made by Anna Lisa Eriksdotter (1794–1875), sewn by hand and padded with fleece on the farm in Sweden where her family have lived since the beginning of the 16th century. The pattern of the centrefield combined with a broad green border gives this quilt a startlingly modern look, but, judging from its early date, it is unlikely that the maker had been influenced by anything other than patterns and styles handed down in Sweden. The wider border is seen on many 19th-century Swedish quilts.

"In our uncertain world we seek our roots, and through the patchwork quilts our past becomes visible." Åsa Wettre, *Old Swedish Quilts*

INTARSIA QUILTING

There are examples of patchwork and wholecloth quilts in Finnish, Swedish, and Norwegian museums, some dating back to the Middle Ages. Two outstanding quilts in the State Historical Museum in Stockholm are early 15th century and are worked in a combination of patchwork and appliqué blocks using a method known as *intarsia*. In this technique, shapes are cut out and inset into a background fabric, and the seams are elaborately embroidered. Such articles are evidence of a long and continuous tradition of fine patchwork and quilting.

Luxurious silk quilts were made for the nobility and there are a number of surviving examples of fine silk quilts, such as a wedding quilt dated 1763 made from embroidered silk patches. As is so often the case, articles made for the upper classes have been preserved for posterity while the rougher covers made by ordinary working people have been worn out and thrown away.

THE SOCIAL STATUS OF QUILTS

From quilt documentation carried out in Sweden and Norway, it is clear that by the end of the 18th century quilts had become common in Scandinavian countries. However, in the very poorest homes, where new garments were a rarity, there would be few remnants from which to make patchwork quilts, so knotted-pile rugs and, in the far north where cold weather conditions were especially severe, animal hides were more commonly used as bed covers until well into the 19th century.

When machine-made cotton fabrics became cheaper quiltmaking gained popularity, and in much of Sweden the possession of large numbers of beautifully made quilts and cushions was considered evidence both of the housewife's thrift and skills, and of the family's standing. Guests were expected to admire the number and quality of the quilts, which would be displayed on beds and chairs.

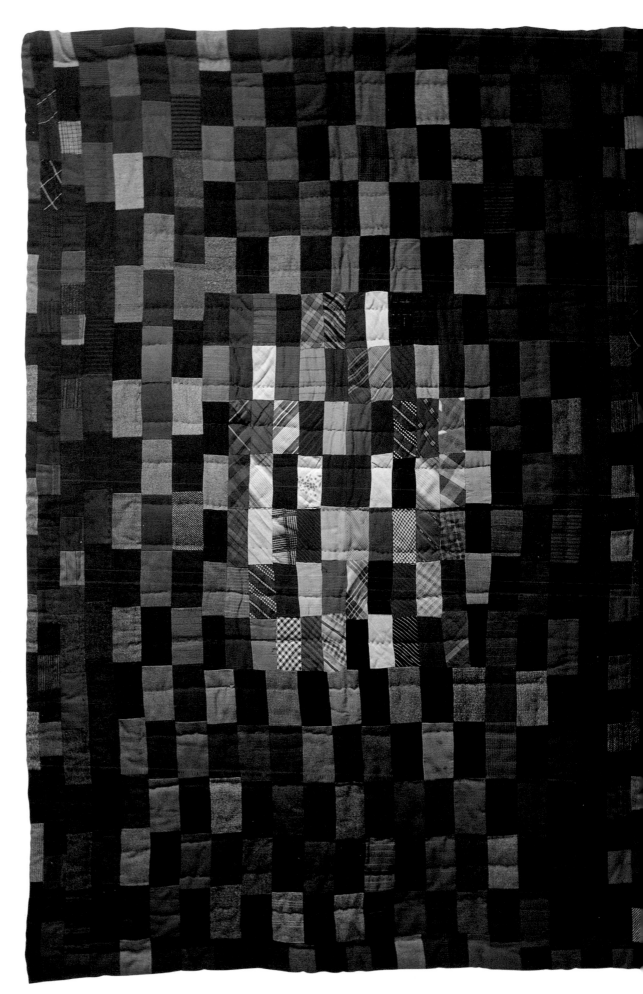

RIGHT   A tailor's quilt made in Sweden by Karl Magnus Jonson, the grandfather of its present owner. Born in 1835 he had five sons, all of whom were taught by him to become tailors. They made clothes for the local people, and from the small pieces left over they created patchwork quilts and pillow covers, sewing everything by hand. This quilt displays a sophisticated aesthetic sensibility in the way in which the more brightly coloured and patterned fabrics have been arranged to create a focal point in what is a very modern-looking design.

AMERICAN INFLUENCES

The best-documented of the Scandinavian quilt traditions is that of Sweden, where extensive research carried out by Åsa Wettre has been published in her book *Old Swedish Quilts*. She indicates that after the great wave of emigration to the USA in 1880–90 there is increasing evidence of the influence of American patchwork and quilting styles and methods brought back by Swedish-Americans. A monthly needlecraft publication for Swedish women, issued in the USA from 1888, suggested patchwork quilting patterns (often taken from popular publications such as *Ladies' Home Journal*), which then spread by way of Swedish magazines, pattern books, and sewing groups. There are, therefore, many examples of quilts made using American patterns dating from this time until the 1930s, when commercially made bedding and blankets became more affordable and interest in quilts began to decline.

The first "sewing bees" were held in Sweden in around 1897; as in the USA, a woman would usually work alone to create the quilt top, but the quilting itself would be a social event as well as a useful source of additional income for spinsters and widows. The remarkable silk patchwork quilt shown right was made in the sort of middle-class home where the women would have worn silk dresses.

LEFT Swedish wedding quilt, 1894, probably made by the bride's mother and inspired by the "crazy" quilt style flourishing in the USA. The patches are embroidered with objects, flowers, and proverbs that give an indication of what was deemed desirable in a middle-class wife, including admonitions to be God-fearing, home-loving, obedient, and hard-working!

RIGHT Silk patchwork quilt sewn at the end of the 19th century by Anne Boethius of Leonardsberg. Embellished with the monograms of her friends, each in its own black silk hexagon, it forms a kind of textile guestbook, and around the edges are mottoes expressing high moral sentiments.

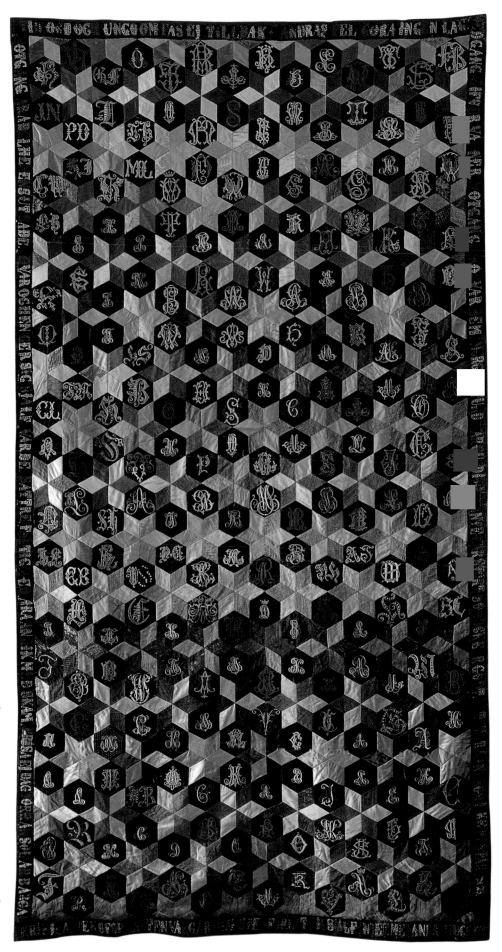

SWEDISH WEDDING CUSHIONS

The whip-stitched cushions traditionally used at Swedish weddings were an important part of the marriage ritual for many years – cushions embroidered with a date as early as 1757 have been found. The custom was for the cushion-bearers to head the wedding procession and, at a certain point, to leave and ride ahead to carry the cushions into the church, after which they would remount their horses, drink to the gathered crowd, and then return to meet the approaching retinue. After the ceremony, the cushion-bearers rode back to the home of the bride to place the cushions where the couple would be sitting. When the wedding was over cushions were also sometimes hung up in the "best" room of the house, one on each side of the window.

Most of these cushions seem to have been made in the Vastbo region, a relatively deprived part of Sweden, and no doubt they gave the inhabitants an opportunity to deploy their ingenuity to make something beautiful out of recycled fabrics. Although today the cushions have faded and appear rather dull, they would once have been bright and colourful additions to the festive scene. The fabric on the reverse often reveals the original colours.

ABOVE LEFT Wedding cushion embroidered with the date 1796. The corners of the cushions were usually decorated with tassels made from square pieces of homespun fabric in different colours, and the backing was of untreated leather hide, with the fur turned inside. Sometimes chamois was used instead.

LEFT Homespun wool or broadcloth fabric was most often used for the patches, which were arranged in geometrical patterns and whip-stitched; in this technique the seams were not turned under – the patches were joined by butting up the edges and then whip-stitching them together. The seams were finished with narrow ribbons.

ABOVE Patterns on the Vastbo wedding cushions were created either around a star of between four and eight points (this example is designed round a six-pointed star), or around a central square. The whip-stitching technique meant that even the smallest pieces of fabric could be used, and single patches were often built up from several smaller pieces, as shown here.

"Queen of the Night" by Maija Brummer, Finland, 2003. A complex quilt surface has been created using a variety of
materials including cottons, velvet, silk, and hand-dyed fabrics, which has then been machine-quilted and embellished.
The artist's inspiration came from gazing at the night sky studded with stars, which she says is for her a spiritual experience.

"Winter Half of the Year" by Katriina Flensburg, Sweden, 1993. A lyrical reflection of the northern Scandinavian winter, which is at once long, cold, dark, and very beautiful. Here winter lasts for about six months, beginning with the golden play of light on trees and landscape before the onset of the truly dark period, when all of nature seems almost dead and the sun barely rises above the horizon.

THE AMERICAN PATCHWORK QUILT, THE SUBJECT OF

MYTH AND LEGEND AND, EQUALLY, OF EXTENSIVE

RESEARCH AND DOCUMENTATION, HAS ACHIEVED

ICONIC STATUS AND, FOR GOOD REASONS, TENDS TO

TAKE CENTRE STAGE AMONG THE QUILTING TRADITIONS

OF THE AMERICAN CONTINENT. BUT IT IS NOT ALONE IN

THE AMERICAS

ITS CONTRIBUTION TO THE IMMENSE RICHNESS AND

DIVERSITY OF BOTH TRADITIONAL AND CONTEMPORARY

QUILTS IN THIS REGION OF THE WORLD; MANY ETHNIC

GROUPS PUT PATCHWORK AND QUILTING TECHNIQUES

TO USE IN A VARIETY OF WAYS, FROM CLOTHING TO

COVERINGS, AND SOME HAVE ENRICHED ENORMOUSLY

THE REPERTOIRE OF TECHNIQUES AND STYLES AVAILABLE

TO CONTEMPORARY QUILTMAKERS.

NORTH AMERICA : HISTORY AND TRADITIONS

"...quilt stories have become myths. As long as quilts provide a tangible link to our family and national heritage, their history will continue to be romanticized." Barbara Brackman, *Clues in the Calico*

In the Europe that the early settlers were leaving behind, quilts were luxury articles affordable only to the wealthy. What was more, given the struggle for survival that they had when they arrived, the early English settlers would not have been creating anything resembling the patchwork quilts that by the 19th century had become such a prominent feature of the American folk art tradition. Quilts surviving from colonial days are predominantly wholecloth, made from wool, cotton, and linen. The first references to patchwork quilts appear only during the

18th century: the word "patched" is used to describe a quilt in Maryland in 1760. About 15 date-inscribed quilts from the 18th century have been identified as having been made in America, four of which are wholecloth and the remainder patchwork, all of which date from after 1770. For many years the famous Saltonstall quilt, named after the family through whom it was said to have descended, was credited as being the oldest American-made patchwork. Thought to date back to 1704, it was cited as an example of the high standard of needlework achieved in America by that time. However, in the 1980s the quilt was re-examined and it was found that although papers on which the patches had been pasted bore the date 1701, and the pattern and style of the fabrics indicated an

ABOVE "Centennial Flags" quilt from the family of Katie Weber of Temple, Pennsylvania. It is apparently a version of the bandanna sold at the 1876 Centennial Exposition featuring the flags of the participating nations. As the popularity of quiltmaking increased, so did the variety of printed fabric designs available, including those that were produced to commemorate specific events, such as the Exposition. Commemorative fabrics are obviously very helpful in the dating of quilts.

RIGHT Cotton appliqué block quilt with a wide border of winding stems, grapes, and vine leaves, c.1850–70. Early quiltmakers, especially the English colonists, cut out motifs from printed chintz fabrics, but during the 19th century this gave way to other appliqué styles – reflecting the diverse national and regional decorative traditions of settlers from Germany, Sweden, and other European countries. The two leaf patterns alternating in this quilt are classic examples of 19th-century designs. Appliqué border designs such as this, both for pieced and appliqué quilts, have remained popular to this day.

18th-century origin, in fact the fabrics appear to date from the mid- to late-19th century. The McCord coverlet, almost certainly made in England and then taken to Canada, is now generally acknowledged to be the oldest dated patchwork quilt on the American continent.

The design format of these early quilts is usually the medallion and borders style so characteristic of English quilts of the time. Written records and surviving quilts suggest that although the American patchwork quilt developed in the 18th century, it did not become widespread until the time of the American Revolution, after which increasing industrialization of the textile industry meant that cotton cloth and thread became

cheaper and more readily available. The notion that colonial homes were furnished with beautiful patchwork quilts is largely a myth, part of the widespread romanticization of the quilt that persists to this day.

Even though quiltmaking, and the social conventions surrounding it, were flourishing during the 19th century, anything written about it tended already to be tinged with nostalgia. Quilts continued to be made in the time-honoured styles, the medallion style retaining its popularity, but as quiltmaking increased the block format began to dominate; the availability of cheaper fabrics gave quiltmakers greater choice of fabrics and colours, and encouraged innovation in quilt patterns and designs.

AMERICAN BLOCK PATCHWORK

During the 19th century the block format, in which a single design is repeated to form the surface of the quilt, gained in popularity. This was partly because blocks are a convenient way of working, being small enough to carry around until there are enough to join together for a quilt top. The popular quilting "frolics" (parties) that 19th-century writers began to record developed into social occasions, providing entertainment as well as a way of expediting the time- and labour-intensive work involved in hand-quilting large bed covers. Nostalgia for these neighbourly parties, with their opportunities for socializing, gossip,

and matchmaking, was probably partly responsible for the romanticization of the quilt and everything surrounding it.

As the century progressed the number of pieced patterns increased, and quilt designs began to appear in magazines. The first published pattern was in *Godey's Lady's Book* in 1835, but pattern publication only really took off in the late 19th century. Exhibits of quilts became a feature of agricultural fairs, and were used for fund-raising activities: many Civil War-era quilts were auctioned for this purpose. Diaries and memoirs of the early 1800s reflect the spread of quilts and quiltmaking into everyday American life.

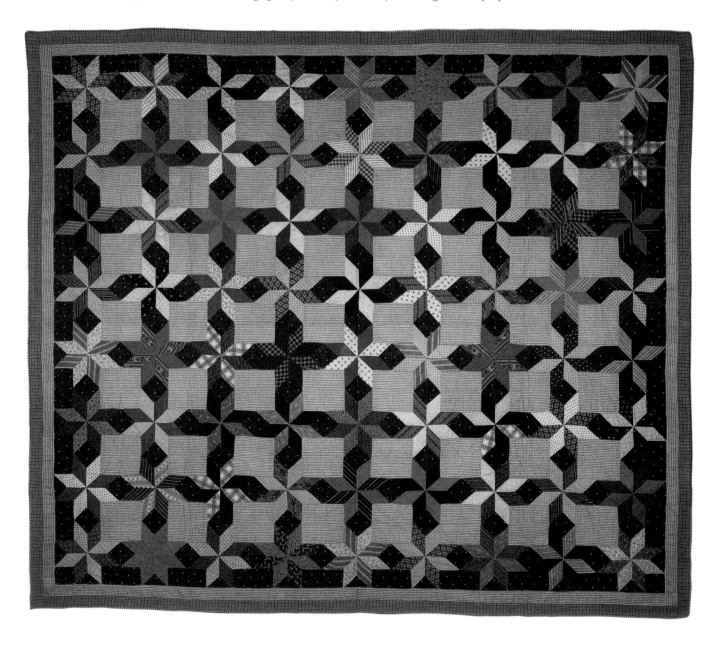

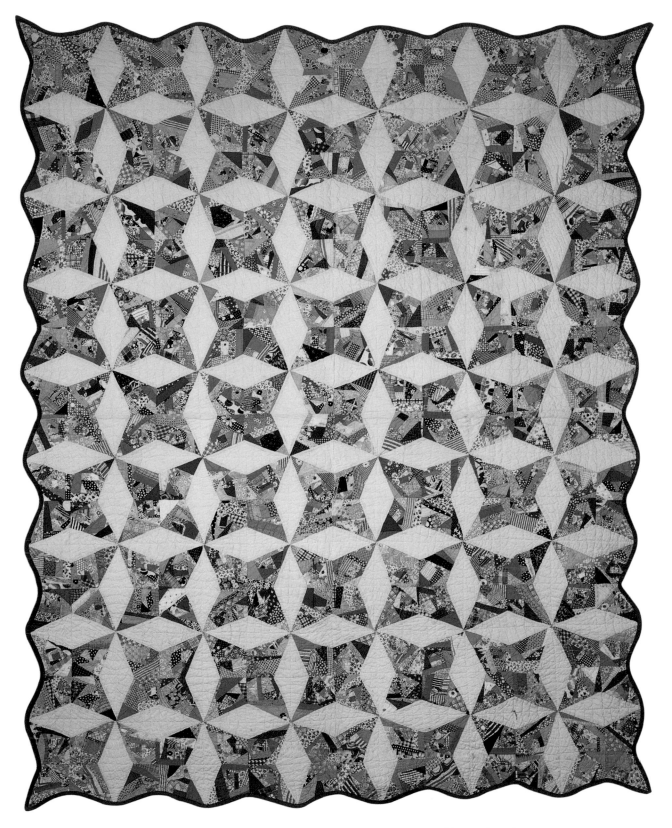

LEFT Scrap quilt, made in Pennsylvania
c.1870, in which four-pointed stars have
been pieced using many different fabrics.
However, the quilt is unified by the strong
graphic effect created by the joined blocks.
The secondary patterns that often emerge
when identical blocks are joined are
a design strength of the block format.

ABOVE "Four Point Stars" block quilt, made
in New York State, *c*.1930, which displays
an instinct for thrift as well as for design.
Small scraps of fabric have been "string-
pieced" together until they are big enough
to be cut out as patches. The cream triangles
join to form diamonds in the background,
and add another dimension to the design.

BLOCK PATCHWORK: METHOD AND STYLE

American patchwork blocks are usually categorized according to the grid on which they are drafted; for example, a "nine-patch" block is drafted on a grid that is three-by-three, or multiples thereof. American patchwork can be worked by hand or, as is now more often the case, by machine. The hand-stitched version differs from English patchwork in that the patches are not basted over papers but are joined with right sides together with a running seam. The block is pieced in units, which are then joined together. Most shapes can be pieced in straight lines, but where there are awkward angles, as in the block above, seams must be "set in".

ABOVE "David and Goliath". This five-patch block was published in a magazine in 1934, but patchwork patterns were often handed down for many years before they appeared in print. Traditional blocks like this were often known by different names in various parts of America. This one is also known as "Doe and Darts", "Flying Darts", and "Four Darts". When repeated blocks of this pattern are joined to make a quilt top interesting secondary effects appear, a perfect example of the design strengths of the patchwork block and one explanation for its perennial popularity.

BELOW "Touching Stars", featuring "Star of Bethlehem" blocks and trapunto quilting, late 19th century. Eight-pointed stars, each blade pieced from diamond shapes, were popular both as central medallions and, as shown here, for block quilts. The triangles at the corners and sides are pieced in plain fabric and join to form squares when blocks are repeated. This design has been adopted by Sioux Indians and other tribes who, for several generations, have specialized in making quilts that comprise a single, large "Star of Bethlehem".

RIGHT "Mariner's Compass", late 19th century. An early mention of a "Mariner's Compass" quilt in a will dated 1798 suggests that this traditional pattern, or at least a pattern of that name, has been around for a very long time. But patterns change over the years, and during the 19th century intricate patterns like this tended to become ever more complicated.

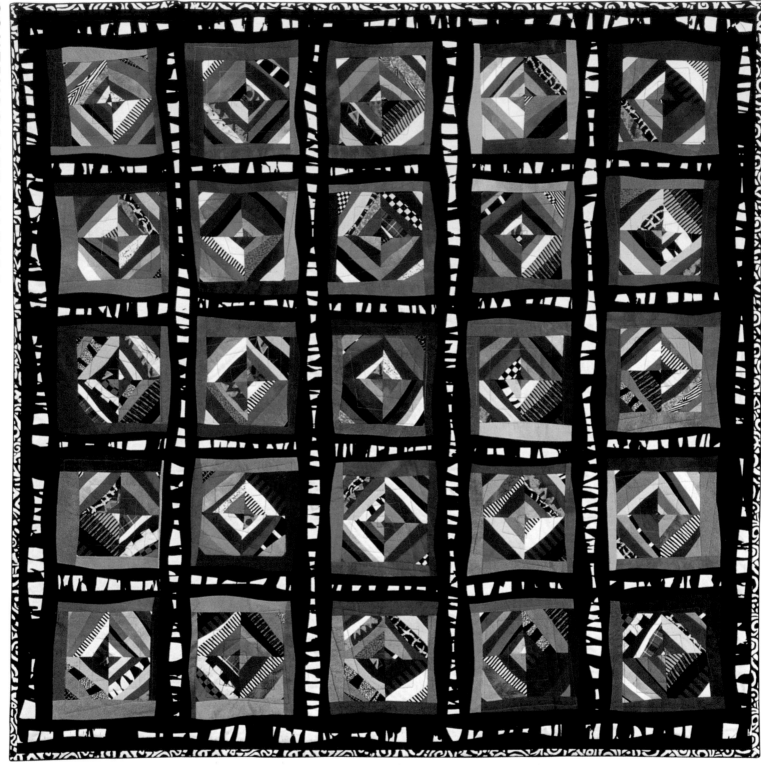

"Ad Lib" by Janet Steadman, 1995. Machine-pieced and machine-quilted, this improvisational quilt was made by cutting strips without the use of rulers or templates. The vibrant colours result from mixing hand-dyed fabrics with commercial prints. The traditional block format has been exploited to organize and give structure to an otherwise free and innovative design.

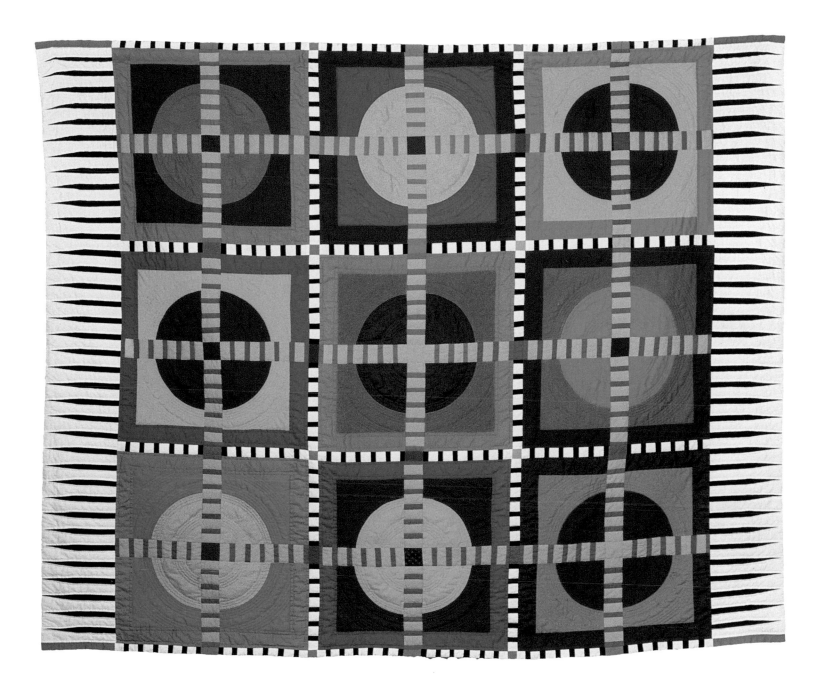

"Manhattan Heatwave" by Elizabeth Cave, 1987. This quilt is also machine-pieced and hand-quilted. Ingenious use has been made of the traditional block, known as "Drunkard's Path", to produce a truly vibrant and exciting quilt. Each block is made from four "Drunkard's Path" blocks joined by striped fabrics, and all blocks are then joined by striped sashings. A layered effect is created so that the pieced blocks seem to be sitting on striped fabric, while a grid of different striped fabric has been placed over them.

AMISH QUILTS

"Amish Quilts are an honest and intimate reflection of a society to which we do not have easy access. Their strong designs and striking colours, arranged in infinite combinations, allow us a glimpse of the richness, vitality, and diversity of the Amish people ..." Robert Bishop and Elizabeth Safanda, *Amish Quilts*

The Amish, or "Plain People", are an Anabaptist sect who emigrated from Germany, first settling in Lancaster County, Pennsylvania, around 1727. Living as farmers and craftsmen in rural settlements and villages, they followed a strict lifestyle based on their Christian beliefs, maintaining their core values of self-reliance and family. They started to make quilts from around 1860, adopting a style that reflected these beliefs. Regarding decoration and ornament as signs of excess, they used solid-colour fabrics dyed at home with plant dyes, which yielded the "saturated" colours so characteristic of early Amish quilts. Once sewing machines came into use, in the latter part of the 19th century, patchwork was usually machine-stitched, while quilting was done by hand communally. Amish communities varied in their degree of conservatism and adherence to plain living, so in some areas quilts were brighter and more intricate.

LEFT "Centre Diamond" quilt in characteristic Amish colours and style. The use of contrasting dark colours is typical of Amish quilts and produces a characteristically brilliant and glowing effect. The large patches allowed plenty of space for fine and beautifully worked quilting patterns, which are a particular glory of the best examples of Amish quilts.

ABOVE "Trip Around the World", also known as "Sunshine and Shadow", which was a very popular design with the Amish. Although it was used by other quiltmakers, the Amish version can be distinguished by the use of plain fabrics. The wide border added to the centrefield displays the sort of fine quilting that was such a distinctive feature of Amish quilts.

AMISH QUILTS: METHOD AND STYLE

The unique colours of early Amish quilts resulted from the fact that Amish women dyed their own cloth, using weeds, berries, and barks. Pieces of clothing or other remnants, usually wool, were thriftily collected and used for quiltmaking – Amish women did not begin purchasing fabrics for clothes and quilts until the end of the 19th century. Quilts were pieced at home but the quilting, done on frames, was usually a communal activity. Cardboard, tin, or even wood templates were used to mark the quilt with motifs such as roses, tulips, or feathers.

ABOVE "Centre Diamond", a characteristically Amish quilt design, surrounded by large, plain rectangles and squares, providing ample space for decorative stitching. Evidence suggests that the patterns of the ornamental quilting on Amish quilts may have been adaptations of appliqué motifs seen in the quilts of their non-Amish neighbours.

RIGHT This unusual eight-pointed star quilt, made in Arthur, Illinois, around 1920, is a superb example of the fine quilting skills of the Amish quiltmakers. The star is pieced from woollen fabric that has been set into cotton sateen.

"Roman Stripe Log Cabin" quilt made in Lancaster County, early 20th century. As Amish communities became more stable, developing a less restrictive way of life, quilt styles also changed. The women began to use brighter and more varied colours and to make pieced quilts in the style of mainstream quilts, even preferring to use polyester and other man-made fibres once they became available. This trend has continued, although many contemporary Amish quilts, such as this one, are still made in traditional colours, and display the superior workmanship for which the Amish are renowned.

"Lone Star" wall quilt in woollen fabric. Although many contemporary Amish quiltmakers now use cotton fabrics almost exclusively, this quilt is made from old woollen fabric, some of which is recycled from old Amish clothing. Early Amish quilts had a very thin batting, making it easier to achieve fine decorative quilt patterns; the very thin batting in this quilt makes reference to that tradition.

APPLIQUÉ QUILTS

Appliqué appears on American quilts dating back to the 18th century. Motifs for early medallion quilts were usually cut from chintz in the style known as *broderie perse*, although original appliqué designs were also created. The appliqué quilt reached its height of popularity toward the middle of the 19th century, just before the Civil War, and was judged by many to be the very epitome of artistry in quiltmaking. After 1840, and for the rest of the 19th century, typical American appliqué quilts featured coloured shapes on a white background – red and green were the preferred colours for the motifs. Elaborate borders consisting of swags, vines, and floral trails were also a common feature. Although the patterns used in this style seem to have emerged in the 1840s without antecedents, most of the motifs can be traced back to the needlework traditions that were an essential part of a young girl's upbringing. Each girl would have been familiar with the designs in Indian *palampores* and Jacobean embroidery, for example, and the multitude of variations on the theme of the rose (such as the "Rose of Sharon", "Whigg Rose", and "Wild Rose") might have been inspired by the stylized Tudor Rose of the English embroiderers.

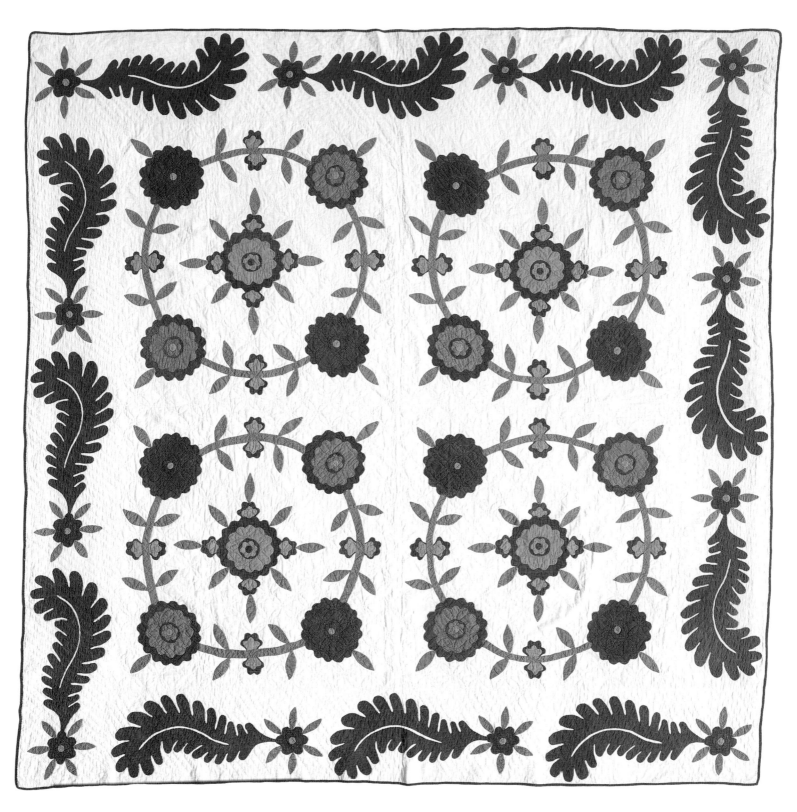

LEFT "Princess Feather" made in York County, Pennsylvania, c.1890. Feathers have been used as quilting motifs for centuries, in England and then in America, and are still popular today. It is likely that the name derives from the Prince of Wales' emblem of three feathers, which was adapted for appliqué on quilts during the early 19th century.

ABOVE "The President's Wreath", 1860. This pattern probably dates back to the early 19th century and is seen in many quilts of the period. During the Civil War it was named in honour of President Lincoln, but it is also known as "Rose of Sharon" and "Wreath of Roses". The blocks are large, so only four are needed when the "Princess Feather" border is added.

APPLIQUÉ QUILTS: METHOD AND STYLE

Appliqué is a very old technique, found in many cultures, which probably evolved from the simple expedient of patching over holes or worn areas of cloth to prolong the life of the material. The style of appliqué in which patterns are cut from printed fabrics and sewn onto a background to create a new design is known as *broderie perse*, and can be traced back to the 17th century in Europe. In America this style is also described as "cut-out chintz" appliqué, and was the most popular technique for appliqué quilts during the 18th and early 19th centuries.

LEFT Chintz "Centre Medallion" quilt dating from around 1830; the design has been built up from pieces cut from a floral chintz. At least six earlier, dated examples of these quilts (1782–99) are recorded in America. Cut-out chintz quilts made before 1840 were usually arranged in the medallion style, seen here, whereas after that date they are more likely to have been worked in blocks. Quilt historians attribute this change to the development of the fashion for block-style album quilts around 1840.

ABOVE RIGHT Central panel of a frame quilt dating from around 1845, featuring both patchwork and appliqué. The centre is built up to form a vase of flowers surrounded by birds and animals. The popularity of cut-out chintz appliqué declined around the time of the Civil War and was replaced by what is termed "conventional" appliqué, in which shapes and designs are no longer cut from chintz fabrics but are made and cut out by the quiltmaker herself.

BELOW RIGHT Detail of the border, pieced from triangles and squares, with appliqué animal and leaf motifs echoing those in the centre of the quilt. Some of the fabrics date back to 1800.

ALBUM QUILTS

In the period after 1840 quilts began to acquire a new significance, as women used them to raise funds, to symbolize or comment on political issues, and to express friendship. Album quilts were often communal projects, made to commemorate or celebrate special events, with several people contributing blocks that might all be identical or of different designs. At first the most frequently used technique for the blocks was appliqué, although later there was also a profusion of pieced patterns. When friends contributed their own, individually designed blocks an element of competition often emerged, as each person tried to contribute something original to the joint project; one theory is that it was this aspiration to originality that contributed to the proliferation of both pieced and appliqué block patterns during the second half of the 19th century.

Related styles, such as signature and autograph quilts, were based on a similar idea – each square or block was made and signed by, or on behalf of, a friend or relative, and might also carry some appropriate message. These quilts became quite a fad, and were an adaptation of the bound paper albums inscribed with verses, drawings, and autographs that had been popular since the 1820s.

LEFT This typical album coverlet, c.1860–70, has no fewer than 80 pieced squares to which appliqué motifs have been added. Different forms of cross motifs are bordered by other symbols such as horseshoes, hearts, and leaves; alternate squares are framed by a border of brown chintz with stylized trailing flowers. The fabrics are predominantly printed cottons and chintz, and appear to date from the early 19th century.

RIGHT "Occupational Album Quilt" from New York State, c.1862. Each block is signed by a member of the Vanderbilt family. The occupations represented appear to include tailoring, shoe-making, upholstery, furniture-making, horse-training, and brewing. Such quilts are a gift to quilt historians since they contain a wealth of dates and information, and can even be of help to people researching family genealogy.

FRIENDSHIP QUILTS

Friendship quilts were made as keepsakes for friends and relatives, sometimes as leaving presents or for special occasions. The blocks were signed and often inscribed with messages. Admirers of a prominent or worthy member of the community, such as a minister or teacher, might make them a "presentation quilt" as a testament to the esteem in which they were held. As for the inscriptions they contain, both high moral sentiments and religious conviction feature prominently. A verse from an album quilt dated 1852, for example, reads: "Should I be parted from thee/Look at this and think of me/May I twine a wreath for thee/Sacred to love and memory", while a young man of Carolina County, Virginia, about to leave to go to college, was given a quilt of which one square reads: "Ask Heaven, Virtue, Health,/But never let your prayer be Wealth."

It is important to remember that many friendship quilts were made in the context of the great migration west during the mid-19th century, hence their greatest vogue was in the 1840s and '50s – decades of major migration on the overland trails to California and Oregon. Many of those joining the wagon trails would never again see the relatives and friends they were leaving behind, so these quilts were poignant and treasured reminders of the people and places of their past.

LEFT Friendship quilt dated 1858. A classic example, perhaps made for someone who was emigrating west, with 36 appliqué blocks, mostly in solid-colour fabrics of red, blue, and green on a white background, with red cotton sashings. Motifs include flowers, musical instruments, fruit, a butterfly, and other decorative appliqué patterns. Many of the squares are signed in embroidery or pen-and-ink, and the central square, with the main inscription to Sarah, is signed "Amanda Birdsell April 20th, 1858".

SAMPLER QUILTS

Sampler quilts are block quilts made up of many different patterns; the blocks are not signed so it is generally assumed that the quilts were made by a single person, rather than communally. The sampler style developed at the same time as the album quilt, and there is so much overlap between the two styles that it is often difficult to distinguish between them. At first the blocks were usually worked using the appliqué technique, although pieced blocks might occasionally be included. Later in the 19th century, pieced block sampler quilts seem to have become more popular as the fashion for appliqué declined.

The popularity of these quilts reflects an interest in patterns and pattern names that had increased enormously by the end of the 19th century, when pattern companies such as the Ladies' Art Company produced and sold hundreds of patterns. It seems that many of the sampler quilts dating from the end of the 19th century were assembled as a record of the maker's file of designs. Some of them were simply sewn together quickly as examples, or were kept to be used as templates, with the name of the design sometimes inscribed in Indian ink in the centre of each block.

BELOW Sampler quilt of 10cm (4in) square blocks, c.1880–90. All the fabrics are silks, and although the quilt contains a wide variety of patterns many of them are simply repeats, suggesting that the quilt may have been made to use up scraps of fabrics recycled from dresses, rather than to document block patterns for reference.

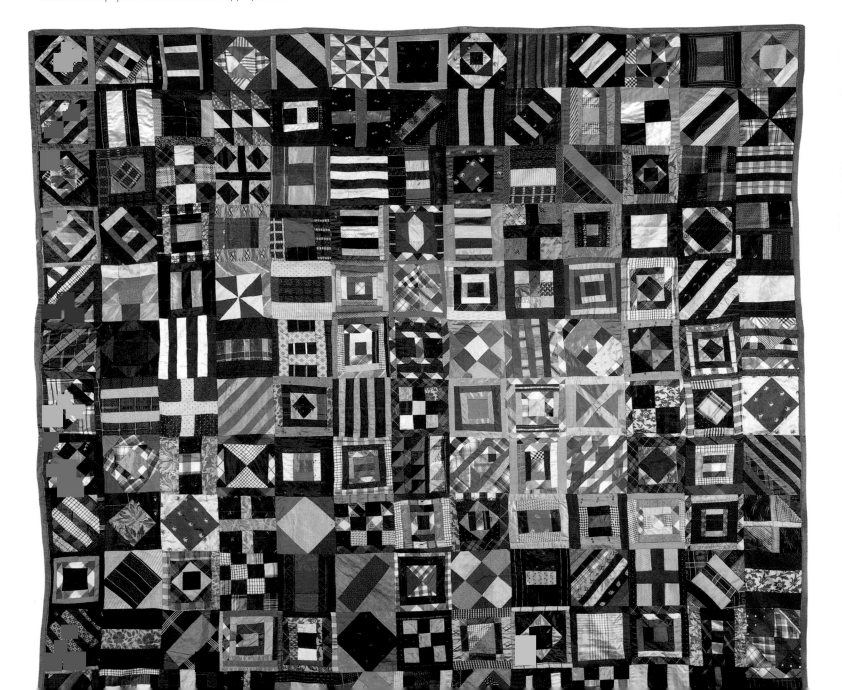

BALTIMORE ALBUM QUILTS

"The most distinguishing characteristic of the finest of these quilts ... is the imaginative manner in which the printed cottons were pieced together to suggest texture, shading, and contour." Dena Katzenburg, *Baltimore Album Quilts*

Although the fashion for album quilts was widespread over the Eastern Seaboard states, the Baltimore album quilt is the epitome of the album style. The quilts made in and around Baltimore in Maryland achieved the height of fashion, each block elaborately appliquéd with a vast range of motifs including floral wreaths, cornucopias, civic monuments, patriotic designs, birds, animals, and even family pets!

The development of this highly decorative form of quiltmaking is largely ascribed to the fact that Baltimore, as the third largest seaport in America at that time, quickly became prosperous, giving rise to a class of women who had leisure, money, and materials to create intricate work. Professional needlewomen also exploited the popularity of the style. The Baltimore album quilt flourished for only a relatively short period, but its influence spread nationwide and enjoyed a revival in the latter part of the 20th century.

LEFT Classic Baltimore album quilt of the 1840s. The blocks have been appliquéd, mostly in red, green, and yellow calico, onto white calico squares, while the centre block has an appliquéd chintz wreath. Three names are signed: Rosina M. Herring, Winifred Smith, and Hannah Ann Robinson. The border is intricately quilted.

ABOVE One of several Baltimore album quilts attributed to Mary Evans, or one of her circle, c.1852. Elaborate appliqué motifs include cornucopias, wreaths, and baskets of flowers, all bordered by swags of flowers and ribbons. The quilting of the group was also of a high standard and often incorporated trapunto, as is the case here.

"Summer House Quilt", hand-appliquéd and machine-pieced by Judy Severson, then machine-quilted by Shirley Greenhoe, 1998. A combination of techniques creates a complex image, based on the traditional "frame" quilt, to produce a contemporary interpretation of traditional styles.

"Jacobean Arbor" by Patricia B. Campbell. The hand-appliquéd blocks echo the style and technique of the Baltimore album quilts, and bear testimony to their continuing popularity and influence, although the inspiration for the design is taken from 17th-century embroidery motifs. An eclectic selection of fabrics has been used; they are predominantly cottons but include others such as hand-dyed silks.

AFRICAN-AMERICAN QUILTS

"Black families inherited this tradition. We forget where it came from because no one continues to teach us. I think we hold to that even though we're not aware of it." Mozell Benson (b. 1934), an African-American quilter, in *Signs and Symbols* by Maude S. Wahlman

There has been much debate about what distinguishes the African-American quilt, and there are almost as many definitions as there are quilt scholars! Some collectors and historians have related the visual character of African-American quilts to jazz, and certainly the two share elements of improvisation and of multiplicity of

patterns and forms. It has also been observed that patterns in African-American quilts reflect the bold designs and colours found in African textile traditions – evident in items such as clothing, tent cloths and bed covers; such quilts are known as "stripe", or "band", quilts and are in made in vibrant colours, often with asymmetrically arranged patterns.

Only two documented quilts surviving from the 19th century can be seen to have discernible African roots, both of which were made by Harriet Powers, who was born a slave in 1837. The narrative ideas, the format, and

ABOVE "Creation of the Animals", c.1886, by Harriet Powers, a famous African-American quiltmaker of Athens, Georgia. This pictorial appliqué quilt depicts 15 biblical scenes, including Adam and Eve in Eden, Jonah being swallowed by the whale, and John baptizing Christ.

RIGHT Quilt made c.1940 by Blanche Ransome Parker, Supervisor of Black Schools in Carroll County, Tennessee. The creative use of colour and design are reminiscent of modern art quilts, but the irregular size, shape, and placement of the blocks are typical of many African-American quilts.

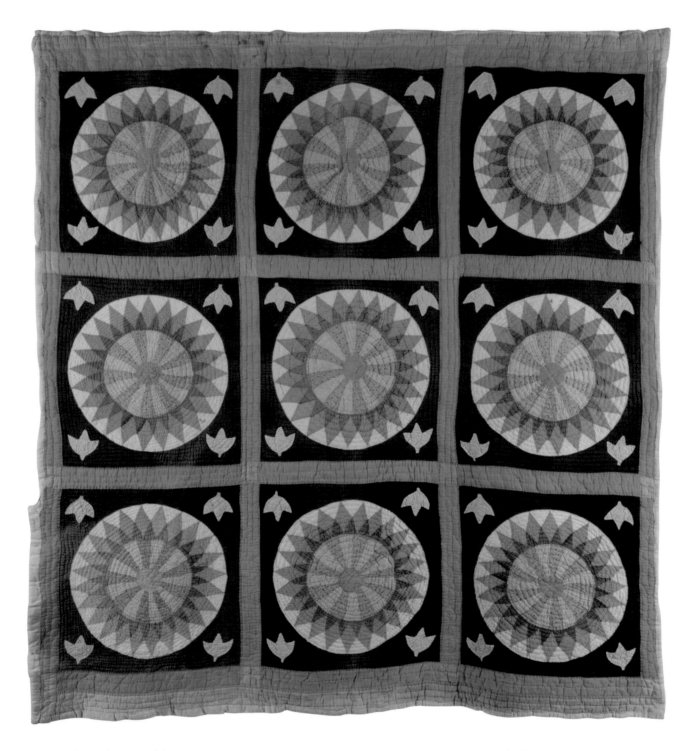

the technique of her quilts can all be related back to the traditional appliquéd tapestries of Dahomey in Western Africa.

Quilts played a special role in the lives of slaves. A network of safe houses existed, known as the "Underground Railroad", where escaping slaves could find refuge during their journey north. Quilts were hung outside the houses to send messages – "Log Cabin" quilts made with black fabric, for example, marked a safe house. Some of the finest needlework of the mid-19th century was executed by slaves, many of whom were employed as seamstresses and nursemaids on plantations. They produced quilts in the patterns they had been taught, and their work reveals a high degree of skill in its execution. As a result, African-American quilts encompass the full range of quilts made in America in the last 200 years, from the traditional patterns of the past to the improvisational quilts of the present, but they remain distinguished by their exuberant, spontaneous use of colour and shapes.

LEFT "The Buzz Saw", made c.1900–20 by Docella Johnson in Bradley, Arkansas, now in the collection of the Old State House Museum. The materials are hand-dyed cottons, sacking, and a little calico. It is quilted 3–4 stitches per inch over a medium batting. Quiltmakers often used familiar tools and implements as design inspiration.

ABOVE African-American strip quilt dating from the 1940s. This rectangular, medallion-style quilt has eight "Roman Stripe" blocks in the centre, surrounded by multiple borders. It is made of a random selection of rayon, gaberdine, and men's shirting fabrics, pieced together in a spontaneous manner reminiscent of contemporary quilt art.

HAWAIIAN QUILTS

"There is no quick method of making a Hawaiian quilt – it requires imagination, deftness and skill." Lenice Ingram Bacon, *American Patchwork Quilts*

The Hawaiian appliqué quilt has become a familiar part of the contemporary quiltmaker's repertoire, and the story behind it is as fascinating as its unique style and design. In March 1820 the first American missionaries dropped anchor in Hawaii. Sewing was deemed to be a suitable and improving occupation for the indigenous population, and the first sewing circle was held in April by the American Board of Missions, who invited the women of the Hawaiian royal household on board ship to teach them how to use scissors and needles. However, Hawaiians already had their own textile tradition: *tapa* was made from the bark of mulberry trees, dyed and pounded with a mallet; with this they made bed coverings and wall hangings. It was therefore a combination of indigenous traditions and quilting techniques brought by the missionaries that gave rise to the unique style and pattern of the now classic Hawaiian quilt. As well as the familiar "Snowflake" style, another, different style achieved a distinctive place in the annals of Hawaiian quiltmaking – namely the flag quilt, known as "Ku'u Hae Aloha" ("My Beloved Flag").

LEFT Hawaiian "Flag Quilt", known as "Ku'u Hae Aloha" ("My Beloved Flag"). The flag of the state was designed before 1816 for King Kamehameha, who placed the islands under the protection of Great Britain. When, in 1893, the Hawaiian Islands became a US territory, the Queen abdicated her throne and the Royal Hawaiian flag was lowered. As the Hawaiians were forbidden to fly their flag thereafter, women expressed their patriotism in quilts that combined images of the Hawaiian flag with those of the British Union Jack.

RIGHT Coverlet dating from the 1920s. This is a brilliant example of the "snowflake" style of Hawaiian quilt, with the border also cut out of a single piece of fabric. The work was not always quilted; this coverlet was neither lined nor wadded, so was probably used as a decorative summer spread. Making a Hawaiian quilt is a labour-intensive task that may take anything from six months to several years to complete.

HAWAIIAN QUILTS: METHOD AND STYLE

The classic Hawaiian appliqué quilt is made from one large appliqué pattern cut from a single piece of folded fabric – the technique is similar to that used for making paper "snowflakes". Solid colours are used for both appliqué and background – usually a white background and a strong contrasting colour, such as red or navy blue, for the appliqué. The coloured design is opened out and pinned to the background fabric, then the edges of the motif are turned under and basted before being whip-stitched to the background. Most Hawaiian quilts are square, with the appliqué covering most of the surface.

ABOVE Inspiration for the motifs is taken from the natural environment and includes plants, animals, and fruits. Patterns belong to specific makers and their families, and have symbolic meanings. A distinctive feature of Hawaiian quilts is the use of "echo" quilting, in which parallel lines of stitching follow the outline of the motif.

RIGHT "Spiraling Hapu'u Tree Ferns" by Lisa Louise Adams, 1999, inspired by living in the lush rainforest of Volcano, Hawaii. An artist who works in many media – as painter, potter, printmaker, bookmaker, paper-maker, and jeweller – Adams began making quilts in 1997 and uses time-honoured methods to express her vision.

CANADIAN RED CROSS QUILTS

"One can imagine that attics were searched and linen cupboards raided to fill the first urgent wartime appeal by the Canadian Red Cross Society." Pauline Adams and Margaret Tucker, *Quilt Treasures: The Quilters' Guild Heritage Search.*

Quiltmaking as part of a war effort can be traced back as far as the American Civil War. Thousands of women saw the provision of quilts and bedding as their contribution to the armed forces, and this tradition was carried on in both world wars, when the victims of war-torn Europe were the beneficiaries of aid from North America. In particular, the archives of the Canadian Red Cross Society show the extent of the aid sent from Canada to European war zones. All the items made and distributed by the CRCS were made to strict patterns, except quilts. This was probably because many of them would have been made before the war, while others were made at home from remnants and quilted in Red Cross sewing rooms. The National Women's War Work Committee chairman, Mrs C. McEachren, OBE, reported: "Nothing has been more popular than the quilts we make and send overseas... large numbers have been distributed both in England and on the continent." It is thought that 25,000 quilts were sent to Europe in just six weeks during 1944.

LEFT Red Cross appliqué "Daisy" quilt in a variety of printed dress fabrics. The quilts appeared in an eclectic range of styles and fabrics, some carefully sewn, others put together quickly and quilted functionally. The blocks in this one have been assembled in a rough-and-ready manner, but nonetheless the result is a warm and colourful quilt, which is still much treasured in its English home!

ABOVE Nine-patch quilt, hand-quilted to a high standard in an all-over diamond pattern. Such quilts were made by hundreds of Canadian women in their own homes for victims of the Blitz. Quilts were also distributed to hospitals and to the armed forces. Many quilts bear the CRCS label (*see* right), although some, believed by their owners to be CRCS quilts, have had their labels removed.

RIGHT The machine-stitched labels on CRCS quilts are attached to one corner on the back, and almost always bear the words "Canadian Red Cross Society", with a red cross in the centre of the label. Sometimes the name of the town and province where the quilt was made is recorded, as in this case; two quilts documented by the Quilters' Guild of the British Isles have labels, one from Edmonton district, Alberta, and one from New Glasgow, Nova Scotia.

CENTRAL AMERICA : HISTORY AND TRADITIONS

"...the panels which they create ... are brilliant artifacts at the very least, or at a high level are folk art of a superior kind." John Canaday, quoted by Betha B. Brown in *Uncoverings: The Journal of the American Quilt Study Group.*

The Kuna Indians of Panama, also known as the San Blas Indians, have made a unique contribution to the contemporary quilt scene, because the distinctive traditional style of appliqué that they use on their costumes is enthusiastically adapted and interpreted by present-day quiltmakers. Rectangular, intricately designed panels are an integral part of the blouses, known as *molas* (a Kuna word that simply means "cloth"), which are part of the traditional costume of the Kuna. The word *mola* is now often used to describe the needlework style rather than the garment itself.

Despite the ever-encroaching influence of Western culture, the Kuna have retained much of their traditional way of life and the *mola* is a unique expression of their independence and pride. In fact, although the style is often described as appliqué, it should more accurately be described as "cut-work stitchery" – a combination of appliqué, patchwork, and needlework embellishment. As for the development of the style, although there is no documentary evidence about the origin of *mola* patterns, one theory proposes that it derives from the art of body painting, which the Kuna were known to have practised from at least the 16th century. The Kuna society is matriarchal and it was observed by early reporters visiting the islands that the women were responsible for carrying out the body art on the men, drawing figures of birds, beasts, trees, and geometrical patterns using brushes made from wood, and pigment that they made themselves from plants and earth. These paintings were important because, according to Kuna beliefs, animals and plants can be inhabited by good or evil spirits and protection from the latter can be achieved by portraying them in tattoos or paintings.

RIGHT The belief that all living creatures originate from the "Earth mother's" womb was the inspiration for this *mola*. In Kuna mythology the Earth mother gave birth to pairs of everything – male and female fitting together perfectly. The symmetry of this superbly worked *mola*, made by a young Kuna man as a Mother's Day gift, expresses perfectly the Kuna people's vision of the world.

LEFT Classic *mola* blouse, 1930s, beautifully worked in geometric designs. *Molas* are made from two rectangular panels attached to a yoke. Rather than a shoulder seam, they have a slit for the head to which the sleeves are attached. The panels are joined to the yoke by embroidered bands, and the sleeves are gathered onto similar bands. The Kuna woman has many *molas*, which are her everyday dress, enabling her to change and wash them frequently.

Women traditionally wore a skirt-like garment, made of hand-woven cotton or, eventually, from fabrics or old clothes obtained from passing traders. In fact, the availability of more colourful cloth as well as needles, thread, and scissors during the late 19th century seems to have been the impetus for decoration of these basic garments, although the intricate "appliqué" technique we now refer to as *mola* seems to have been an indigenous development. It would seem that, once again, this needlework art is a fusion of native cultural traditions and outside influences, resulting in a unique form of decorative folk art.

No one is sure when the first *mola* blouses were made, but the oldest example still in existence was discovered in 1909. Inevitably, the Kuna Indians' increasing exposure to other cultures had an effect on the repertoire of subject-matter depicted in the *molas*, which expanded to include illustrations of current events, and interpretations of Kuna folklore, as well as scenes from everyday life, and, after the arrival of the missionaries, images taken from Christian iconography. The *mola*-maker of today still copies favourite old designs, records events of importance, and, through his or her creation, expresses feelings and personal interests.

MOLAS: METHOD AND STYLE

The front and back panels of the Kuna blouse are made of two or three layers of coloured cotton cloth, measuring about 36cm (14in) by 46cm (18in). The first step is to baste together two layers of differently coloured cloth on which the outline of the design is cut through from the top layer, leaving a silhouette of the motif. The edges of the top layer are neatened by tucking them under and stitching them to the bottom layer, which, if the work is completed at this stage, will make a two-colour *mola*.

ABOVE *Mola* with a stylized representation of a tortoise, dating from 1975. The technique used for making *molas* is often referred to nowadays as "reverse appliqué". If a third layer is to be added, the design is cut out in the same way as before, and the edges are turned under and stitched down, this time leaving a narrow border of the second colour to frame the motif.

RIGHT Detail of "Sea Creatures" *mola*. A *mola* may be completed with traditional appliqué, inlays, colour inserts, and other needlework embellishments, but in a good-quality *mola* the only evidence of stitching should be seen on the reverse. In this example the yellow lines are the base fabric showing through the black top layer. All the other figures are coloured sections applied to the black layer.

"Hocus Pocus" by Charlotte Patera, 1991. The artist says, "I tried to re-invent the *mola*." Using one basic *mola* design, she has found ways to vary it by using striped fabrics, either vertically or horizontally, for the top or bottom layers. Some of the underlayers are pieced with different colours and some of the blocks have circles inserted between the layers.

"Tanz der Nachtschwärmer" by Christel Walter, 1998. The artist has developed a unique, European interpretation of the traditional *mola* technique, because the colours and images used here refer to a European cultural context. Using predominantly silk fabric, the quilt is entirely hand-sewn in the traditional manner. The use of *mola* technique has had a significant influence on contemporary quiltmakers all around the world, who exploit the graphic potential of the negative/positive shapes that are an intrinsic feature of the technique.

Wild Swan

The White Hart

EARLY AUSTRALIAN QUILTS TELL US A GREAT DEAL ABOUT

THE 19TH-CENTURY PATCHWORK AND QUILTING TRADITIONS

OF THE COUNTRIES FROM WHICH THE SETTLERS ARRIVED:

PREDOMINANTLY ENGLAND AND IRELAND, BUT ALSO

WALES. LATER, IMMIGRANTS FROM PAKISTAN, GREECE,

AND ITALY ALSO BROUGHT QUILTS FROM THEIR

COUNTRIES, BUT IT IS THE BRITISH INFLUENCE THAT IS

AUSTRALIA AND NEW ZEALAND

MOST FREQUENTLY SEEN IN SURVIVING QUILTS FROM

THE EARLY 19TH CENTURY. IN NEW ZEALAND, TOO, 19TH-

CENTURY QUILTS REFLECT THE TRADITIONS AND STYLES

OF THE EARLY SETTLERS' COUNTRIES. BUT EUROPEAN

TRADITIONS WERE BY NO MEANS THE ONLY INSPIRATION

FOR EARLY QUILTMAKERS – THE AUSTRALIAN ABORIGINES

HAD THEIR OWN UNIQUE VERSION OF PATCHWORK IN

THE FORM OF FUR RUGS PIECED FROM ANIMAL SKINS.

AUSTRALIA : HISTORY AND TRADITIONS

"...although the Australian decorative arts, 'pottery, furniture, silver', began to show indigenous symbols such as kangaroos, emus, and native flowers as early as the 1840s, upperclass Australian quiltmakers remained firmly rooted in their English origins." Annette Gero, *Historic Australian Quilts*

The earliest documented evidence of patchwork and quilting in Australia comes from the now-famous accounts of the patchwork quilts made by women arriving during the early 19th century on the convict ships. From 1817 to 1843, the Quaker prison reformer Elizabeth Fry supervised the women who were about to depart on the long and arduous voyage to Australia, travelling in appallingly primitive and crowded conditions. She organized a supply of the materials and tools for making patchwork, with the intention that they would have both an occupation for the journey and something to sell on arrival so that they would not be completely destitute. It is recorded that each convict woman was provided with a Bible, two aprons, one small bag of tape, 1 oz of pins, 100 needles, nine balls of sewing cotton, 24 hanks of coloured thread, one small bodkin, one thimble, one pair of scissors, and 2 lbs of patchwork pieces.

Although the scheme was deemed successful, it is known that many of the quilts never reached Australia because they were sold at ports en route, or on arrival in Sydney. All but one of these have vanished without trace. The surviving quilt was made on board *The Rajah*, which sailed for Van Diemen's Land on 5 April, 1841; curiously it was found in Scotland during the 1990s, and was then acquired by the National Gallery of Australia, Canberra.

Of course, not all the women settling in Australia were convicts; many simply came to find a better life. Families who sailed to Australia before the 1860s had to take with them everything for the voyage as well as every household item required for settlement, including bedding and patchwork quilts. As a result, there are many surviving examples of quilts made in England in Australia's museums and galleries, and in private collections.

LEFT "The Rajah Quilt", 1841. The inscription embroidered on the outer border reads: "To the Ladies of the convict ship committee. This quilt, worked by the convicts of the ship *The Rajah* during their voyage to Van Diemen's Land, is presented in gratitude for the ladies' concern for their welfare, both in England and during the passage, and also as proof that they have not neglected their advice to be industrious."

PREVIOUS PAGE Detail of "The Wedding Quilt", made by Mary Jane Hannaford around 1922. This is one of five inspiring folk-art quilts made by Mary when she was in her eighties, based on a workbook of drawings and poems completed in 1861 when she was only twenty. Mary arrived in Australia with her parents when she was two years old and her quilts, embellished with sequins and glass beads, display a uniquely Australian character and humour.

RIGHT "Mrs Keen's Quilt", c.1879. This is one of the very few examples in Australia, other than the "Log Cabin" quilts, of a 19th-century quilt with repeating blocks. This magnificent patchwork comprises 11,000 patches, each one sewn over paper in the English style. Hundreds of small squares are pieced to make larger squares in the centre of the quilt, surrounded by borders on which cats, hearts, and horses have been appliquéd, the horses complete with embroidered bridles! Many fabrics were used, including silks and cottons, probably leftovers from Elizabeth Keen's work, as she was described as a dressmaker on her marriage certificate.

From the diaries of early Australian women we know that as society developed, and economic and social conditions improved, the making of patchwork quilts came to be regarded as a suitable occupation for the middle classes, as it had been in Victorian England. Quilts were displayed at fairs and exhibitions, in much the same way as was happening in America at that time.

Australia has a rich heritage of patchwork quilts from the 19th century, although there is no evidence that quilting involved any of the social activities that became associated with it in America, such as "quilting bees" and "frolics" (see page 134). The women of the early colonies made needlework of the type that was fashionable in England at that time, so there is an abundance of central medallion quilts, hexagons, crazy quilts, and tumbling blocks, many of which have been handed down as treasured heirlooms. In America the characteristic medallion quilt soon gave way to the block style, but in Australia it persisted well into the Victorian era, when crazy quilts became the fashion. Indeed, apart from the "Log Cabin" block style, quilts made from repeated blocks were not often made in Australia until the 20th century.

QUILTS 1900–1970

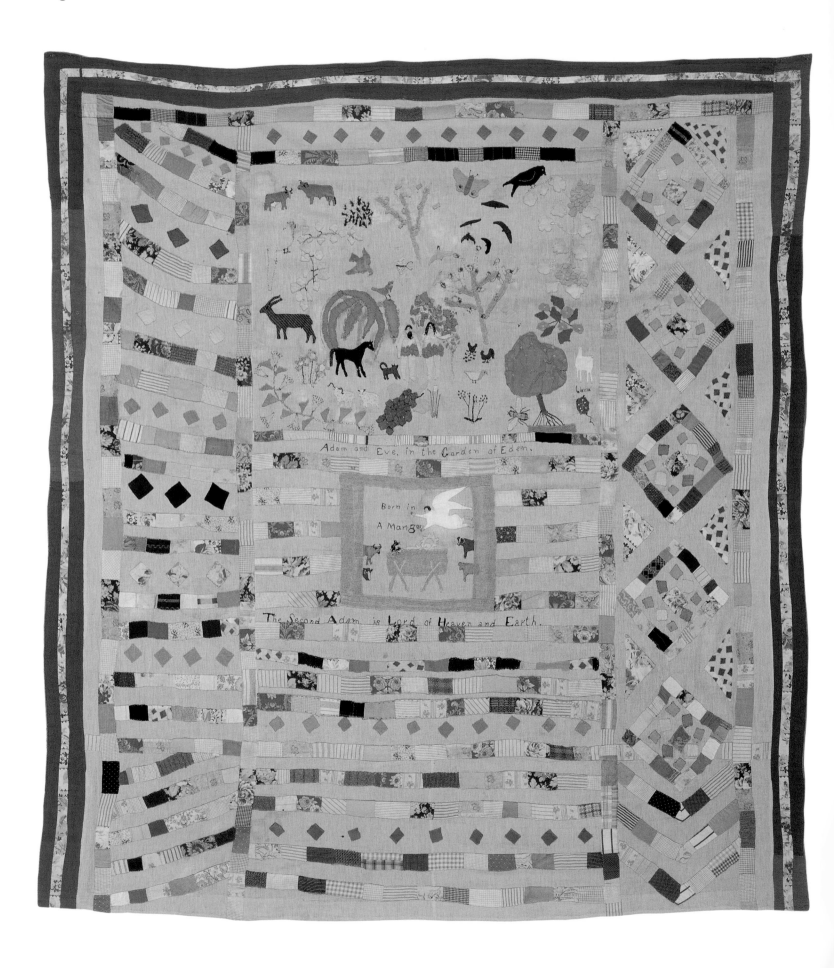

Until the advent of the American-influenced quilting boom in the 1970s, quilts made during the 20th century continued to reflect traditional British styles, with crazy quilts and "Log Cabin" quilts still much in vogue. The advent of World War I, in which thousands of Australian and New Zealand soldiers fought and died, resulted in the production of large numbers of quilts for the armed forces. The Australian Red Cross raised money by organizing the making of signature quilts: people paid to have their names embroidered, usually in red stitching, on squares of white calico. Many examples still survive today.

The years following World War I, which saw the Great Depression, proved very harsh for many working people, so patchwork became an occupation with the dual purpose of making something useful from nothing by using up fabric scraps, while at the same time creating something to enhance the home. There are some very fine examples of both crazy and "Log Cabin" quilts from the 1940s, made from army uniforms and other clothing remnants. During World War II the Red Cross was again active in organizing the making of their characteristic red-and-white signature quilts to raise funds.

LEFT "Adam and Eve in the Garden of Eden" by Mary Hannaford, 1921–30. Mary Hannaford was one of Australia's most creative quiltmakers. Her religious beliefs, love of nature, and patriotism are recurring themes in her quilts. Here, the pieced and appliqué motifs surrounding the biblical scenes are embellished with beads and sequins for the animals' eyes.

RIGHT An intriguing coverlet, c.1941–70, featuring 54 badges from schools in New South Wales. The badges are appliquéd onto squares of woollen fabric, probably store samples, that have been machined together. The edges of the dark cherry wool backing have been folded over to form a border. This is a variation on an earlier style wherein embroidery was added to simple pieced woollen or cotton squares.

WAGGA WAGGAS

LEFT Domestic *wagga* dating from the 1930s. It is made of woollen suiting fabrics, tied with tufted knots of rust-coloured cotton thread. Suiting samples were obtained from tailors and drapers, where men's suits were ordered from sample books. Such patchwork bed covers were usually called rugs, and despite their undeniably functional intention they almost always show evidence of the care that has gone into the arrangement of the colours to make a pleasing effect.

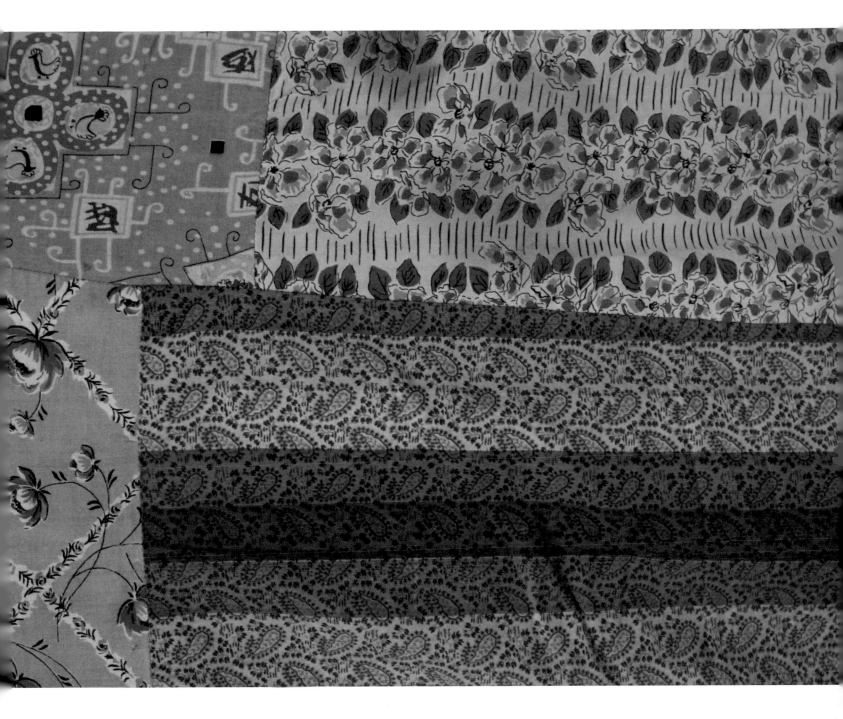

The utility quilt, known variously as a *wagga*, "Bush Rug", or "Bluey", has become something of an icon among contemporary quiltmakers, embodying as it does the spirit of pragmatism and determination of people who survived in difficult and deprived circumstances. It is thought that the term *wagga wagga* derives from the town of that name in New South Wales. This was a centre for wheat production, where there would have been a ready supply of jute wheat bags used by male workers as crude, makeshift covers for camping out when droving, sheep-shearing, or fencing. The bags

were simply opened out and stitched together roughly using twine.

Women made *waggas* for the home by flattening out old clothes or bedding and stitching them roughly onto a foundation of some sort, such as hessian or old blankets. This might then have been covered with a cheap cotton fabric, perhaps made from simple patchwork. Although the name is uniquely Australian, functional bed coverings made in this way were found in other parts of the world, including the north of England and Scotland, where similarly makeshift quilts were referred to as "haps".

CHANGI QUILTS

There are few more poignant memorials to the suffering and privations endured during World War II than the three quilts made by women interned at the Changi jail in Singapore between 1942 and 1945. The quilts are a moving testament not only to the unquenchable courage and optimism shown by those women but also to the importance of needlework in women's lives down the ages.

Ethel Mulvaney, a Canadian who was the unofficial Red Cross leader in the women's camp, first had the idea of making the quilts, which would not only have practical value but also be a means of communication with the men in the big military camps nearby. Squares of white fabric were given out and the women embroidered them, putting "something of themselves" into them and adding their name. Naturally, the quality of the embroidery varies. Eventually three quilts were made, each with 66 squares, and a message was stitched onto the back: "Presented by the women of Changi Internment Camp 1942 to the wounded Australian [British/Nipponese] soldiers with our sympathy for their suffering. It is our wish that on cessation of hostilities this quilt be presented to the Australian [British/Japanese] Red Cross Society. It is advisable to dry clean this quilt."

The quilt for the Japanese was made with the idea that if they expressed equal sympathy for their captors, their quilts would be allowed to reach the hospital in the big Changi military POW camp. The strategy must have worked, because a British military doctor reported seeing the quilts at the camp.

ABOVE The Changi quilt for the Australian soldiers. Embroidered on the quilts for the Australian and British prisoners were patriotic images and "V For Victory" signs, uplifting messages ("Hope Springs Eternal In the Human Breast"), as well as humour and irony. One square depicts a brick wall with the words "Changi holiday home"!

RIGHT The Changi quilt made for the Japanese soldiers. This differs from the other two: it has a greeting in Japanese in the top left corner and most squares are embroidered with flowers and motifs such as the sun rising over water, or an oriental bridge, which the women hoped might please the soldiers.

NEW ZEALAND : HISTORY AND TRADITIONS

"Some families did bring quilts with them, and some women did work on their patchwork quilts on the long, often dangerous journey. But the toil involved in setting up a home and eking out an existence in the new colony does not appear to have provided women with enough leisure time for making quilts, other than simple utilitarian ones..." Pamela Fitz Gerald, *Warm Heritage*

The story of the patchwork quilt in New Zealand is very similar to that of Australia, although by the time settlers were arriving in significant numbers factory-made blankets were readily and cheaply available, and probably used as bed covers. Certainly, records show that woollen blankets were popular items of barter with the Maori people.

It is evident from the quilts made in New Zealand during the early 19th century that, as in Australia, their makers replicated the styles and techniques of their homelands. They contain an eclectic range of fabrics, in many cases remnants from dressmaking and other

LEFT Paisley quilt believed to have been made by Jean Callender, who arrived in New Zealand in 1848. It is made from the lightweight Paisley woollen fabrics in a simple design that uses strips of fabric in a way that echoes the traditional medallion style of English quilts.

RIGHT "Spider Web Quilt". Hexagons pieced in traditional English style have been imaginatively arranged to create an impressive visual effect. Fabrics have been selected in subtle shades of coffee and pale duck-egg blue. The coverlet, displaying skilled use of an "all-over" pattern, was made in Scotland by David Ross and taken to Dunedin in New Zealand by his granddaughter in 1867.

needlework projects. Beside the familiar hexagon quilts, pieced over papers in the English style, which were by far the most popular pattern, the most common pattern in New Zealand is the "Log Cabin". This pattern has its roots in antiquity, and acquired its now familiar name only when it reached North America. Many surviving examples of New Zealand "Log Cabin" quilts are made from shirting cottons, suggesting that the quilters had access to factory offcuts.

TIVAEVAE OF THE COOK ISLANDS

In the Cook Islands, as elsewhere in Polynesia and in Hawaii, an ancient method of producing cloth involved stripping a sapling of its outer bark, then soaking and beating the bark to make a strong and flexible fabric. The resulting material, called "*tapa* cloth", was then elaborately decorated and patterned by stencilling. This craft tradition was eventually superseded when the missionaries arrived on the Cook Islands in the early 19th century and taught sewing skills such as embroidery and patchwork to the inhabitants. Quilts, known as "*tivaevae*", then evolved to become a distinctive Cook Islands style, combining the patterns used on *tapa* cloths with the patterns and methods learned from the Europeans. *Tapa* cloth is still produced, but has been supplanted as a traditional gift for ceremonial occasions such as weddings and funerals, by the *tivaevae*. However, this is not the only use for *tivaevae*: they are just as important in the daily lives of Cook Islands women, for whom making them is a communal activity.

Tivaevae feature a combination of patchwork and appliqué, and there are three distinct styles. *Tivaevae taorei* are the most precious kind, made from tiny pieces of coloured cloth, sometimes numbering thousands,

pieced together to form a colourful mosaic on which more patterns are created by applying separate pieces of fabric, which may be richly embroidered. The second kind, *Tivaevae manu*, use only two colours, the pattern being folded, cut, and then appliquéd to the background, very much in the manner of Hawaiian quilts (*see* pages 162–5). Finally there are *Tivaevae tataura*, which combine appliqué with embroidery: floral motifs are elaborately decorated with a variety of stitches and then appliquéd to a plain background.

LEFT Ceremonial *Tivaevae tataura* thought to date from the 1940s. *Tivaevae* have had a profound effect on the women who make them, because their creation has now evolved into a distinctive art form through which creativity and ideas can be expressed. They have supplanted the traditional *tapa* cloths as tokens of love and friendship, and as decorative coverings used on ceremonial occasions.

RIGHT A classic *Tivaevae manu*, made in the 1990s. The top layer is made by folding it four or eight times and cutting out the pattern in a "snowflake" design. As in Hawaiian quilts, shapes of locally growing plants and leaves are popular motifs. The cutting of complex designs such as this is often entrusted to experts in the technique, known as *taunga*.

CONTEMPORARY MAKERS

"Bush Textures" by Wendy Lugg, 1994. The Australian landscape was the inspiration for this and many of the artist's early works. Here, simple string piecing is supplemented by overprinting with a variety of marks to interpret the subtle colours and textures of the Australian bush.

"Rata Glow II" by Marge Hurst, 2002. The glowing colours of the New Zealand wild flower rata (*Metrosideros*) are the inspiration for this quilt. The artist says: "More than ten years ago I made a quilt out of my imagination showing the rata in bloom in the mountains. I still have not seen the rata in bloom and have used my imagination again to make this quilt."

THE SYMBOLIC IMPORTANCE OF PATCHWORK CLOTHING,

WORN AS A SIGN OF POWER AND SPIRITUAL VIRTUE, IS NOT

CONFINED TO ASIA: IT IS ALSO EVIDENT IN MANY PARTS

OF WEST AND NORTH AFRICA. IN GHANA, FOR EXAMPLE,

THE SUPERIORITY OF CHIEFS OF CERTAIN TRIBES WAS

REPRESENTED BY THE PATCHWORK AND APPLIQUÉ ROBES

THEY WORE. EVEN AT THE BEGINNING OF THE 20TH

AFRICA

CENTURY, LIBERIAN CHIEFS STILL WORE GARMENTS

FASHIONED FROM DYED LEATHER, WHICH WAS PIECED

INTO ELABORATE PATCHWORK PATTERNS. AFRICA'S TEXTILE

HERITAGE IS AS RICH AND DIVERSE AS THE CONTINENT

ITSELF. ALTHOUGH IN MANY WORLD CULTURES WOMEN

PLAY THE MAJOR ROLE IN THE PRODUCTION AND

APPLICATION OF TEXTILES, IN MUCH OF AFRICA IT IS

THE MEN WHO ARE PREDOMINANT IN THIS FIELD.

AFRICA : HISTORY AND TRADITIONS

"Patchwork clothing as a privilege of the ruling class, however anachronistic that may strike us, is found again and again, not only in Asia but also in West and North Africa."
Schnupp von Gwinner, *The History of the Patchwork Quilt*

In 1820 a collection of gifts sent to King George IV of England by the chief of the Asanti included a battle dress in the form of a cotton robe covered with scraps of cloth and Arabic lettering. However, it is reliably reported that it could withstand a blow from a steel weapon as well as the recoil of a flintlock gun. Further evidence that patchwork and quilted armour was used well into the 19th century comes in an account given by a German explorer travelling in North and Central Africa between 1849 and 1855, who reports that both men and horses in the army of the ruler of Bornu wore quilted armour. A wonderful example of patchwork and quilted horse armour from Sudan is on display in the Museum of Mankind in London.

The rich textile tradition of North Africa, which includes weaving and embroidery, is well known, but the appliqué found on the tents and wall hangings in Morocco and Cairo must surely count among the most spectacular examples of textile art in the world. Elaborate appliqué patterns are built up in small segments, in much the same way as the Moorish tilework that the appliquéd tent hangings imitate in style and colour, complete with arabesques and Arabic calligraphy. Tents are made for social occasions, such as feasts, weddings, and funerals, and the brightly coloured hangings used to decorate them are an important feature.

Today, advances in fabric printing technology mean that machine-made reproductions of the patterned tent cloths are easily and cheaply available, and are widely used throughout North Africa for practical, decorative, and ceremonial purposes. Despite this, in Egypt at least, the continuous tradition of tent-making (an exclusively male occupation) survives, and in recent years has been supported by an increase in tourism that has created a demand for authentically made local crafts.

The tent-makers of Cairo work in the Shariah-el-Khamia ("Street of the Tent-Makers"). They are the descendants of the original tent-makers, and still use methods and patterns that have been handed down from generation to generation. The designs are a combination of motifs and symbols dating from Pharaonic times and Islamic decorative styles. Stylized figures depicting scenes from the *Egyptian Book of the Dead*, and versions of the lotus flower, symbol both of Upper Egypt and of rebirth, are also popular. The designs are transferred to cloth by "pouncing": they are drawn and pricked out with a blunt needle on brown paper, which is then placed over the background fabric and sprinkled with charcoal dust. The pattern, thus transferred, is then gone over with a pencil. The background fabric is then basted onto a heavy canvas backing. Each piece is roughly cut and manipulated to fit the appropriate shape on the background fabric, the rougher edges being turned under with the needle as it is slip-stitched to the background.

PREVIOUS PAGE Leather patchwork garment of a Liberian chief, dating from the early 20th century and displaying many elaborate patchwork patterns. In Africa, as in Asia, patchwork and appliqué clothing symbolized power and prestige, and signified that the wearer was acknowledged as "the greatest".

RIGHT Appliqué tent hanging dating from the first half of the 20th century. This superb hanging is an example of the way in which traditional Islamic designs are interpreted in this medium. The design and motifs relate to the intricate ceramic tile patterns used to decorate buildings, especially palaces and mosques, and to patterns used for prayer mats; here, as in the prayer mats, the arch refers to and echoes the shape of a *mihrab* – an alcove or niche indicating the direction of Mecca found in every mosque.

LEFT Cotton appliqué panel, c.1960s, intended for domestic use. It was made in the famous Street of the Tent-Makers in Cairo, where today many such items are produced for the tourist market. Originally a limited palette of colours, mainly primary colours, was used in the appliqué, each with its own symbolism: red signified strength and happiness, green was for health and prosperity, blue for the colour of heaven, and black for fertility and rebirth.

"Egyptian Splendour" by Tarok Fattoh, 2004. The artist is a descendant of one of the original Cairo tent-makers who have been established in the Shariah-el-Khyamia ("Street of the Tent-Makers") since the 14th century. At its height, tent-making occupied no fewer than 8,000 skilled craftsmen in and around this location; today there are only about eight families still working. Tarok Fattoh was taught to stitch by his great-grandfather, and this quilt is a contemporary interpretation of the traditional style, using as its central focus the lotus, the symbol of rebirth, which is the predominant motif in tent hangings.

"Bongewefela" by Sally Scott, April 2004. *Bongewefela* is a Tswana word meaning "unity". The artist was born in Zimbabwe and her childhood was spent on a farm near the Nyanga Mountains. This quilt is a celebration of her awareness and appreciation of the beauty of the natural environment of rural Africa and of its people, captured in the colours and patterns she has used. She says: "It is a celebration of life and love and the power of the human spirit".

THE CONTEMPORARY PASSION FOR QUILTMAKING HAS

BEEN FUELLED PRIMARILY BY INFLUENCES FROM THE

USA, BEGINNING IN THE EARLY 1970S WITH A TOURING

EXHIBITION, "ABSTRACT DESIGN IN AMERICAN QUILTS",

ORGANIZED BY JONATHAN HOLSTEIN AND GAIL VAN

DER HOOF. SINCE THEN QUILTMAKING HAS BECOME A

GLOBAL PHENOMENON, EVOLVING INTO A DISTINCTIVE

INTERNATIONAL GALLERY

TEXTILE ART IN WHICH MANY PEOPLE, PREDOMINANTLY

WOMEN, FIND A UNIQUE MEDIUM FOR PERSONAL

EXPRESSION. ANOTHER RESULT OF THIS REAWAKENED

INTEREST IN QUILTS HAS BEEN TO STIMULATE RESEARCH

INTO MANY PREVIOUSLY NEGLECTED NATIONAL QUILTING

TRADITIONS. THIS INTERNATIONAL GALLERY PRESENTS

A BRIEF OVERVIEW OF SOME OF THE MANY WAYS IN

WHICH THE QUILT HAS DEVELOPED SINCE THE 1970S.

"Hell's Granny" by Dorothy Stapleton, England, 2003. Made to celebrate the artist's 60th birthday, this quilt expresses her exuberant defiance of the inexorable ravages of time! Many of her quilts are quirky comments on concerns in the life of the average woman: "There's more to life than housework" and "Only spring clean when Granny's due to visit" appear on one of her quilts. As for mistakes, her philosophy is: "In life, as well as in quilting, difficulties and disasters can be made into opportunities with a bit of lateral, creative thinking".

"Medieval Strippy II" by June Barnes, England, 2002. A contemporary interpretation of the traditional strippy quilt, typical of a style found mainly in the north of England (*see* pages 72–3). The designs within the strips, inspired by medieval patterns, are quilted and then enhanced with appliqué and trapunto. The completed quilt was repeatedly dyed to achieve the antique effect. The quilt exemplifies the eclecticism of contemporary quilt artists, who take their design inspiration from sources ancient and modern, and call on a variety of techniques to realize their vision.

"Galston, Isle of Lewis" by Effie Galletly, England, 2004. This is the third in a series of quilts inspired by the light and colours of the islands of the Outer Hebrides in Scotland. An impressionistic image is created purely from shapes and colours that reflect those of the landscape. She used the block format to convey the subtle range of colour and light seen in pebbles, sand, weeds, and sky, and the speed with which colour and light can change.

"Mullaghmore Reflections" by Ann Fahy, Ireland, 1996. Mullaghmore is a rocky outcrop in the limestone pavement area known as The Burren in the west of Ireland, an endangered area of natural beauty, constantly under threat from developers, that the artist seeks to celebrate and record in her quilt. Fabric manipulation creates the tactile quilt surface that she feels is especially appropriate for suggesting landscape and organic forms. The hill, with its reflection, forms a shape that could also be seen as a weapon, giving the quilt another layer of meaning.

"Nocturnal Garden" by Ted Storm-van Weelden, Netherlands, 2001. This design is based on Holland's black Delftware, less well known than the famous blue Delftware but in fact made by the same company, De Porcelyn Fles. The artist says that the quilt reflects a period in her life of contrasting experience, "dark, yet rich". It is hand-appliquéd, hand-embroidered, and hand-quilted. It also features trapunto technique and is embellished with beads and small mirrors of the sort used in some Indian quilts.

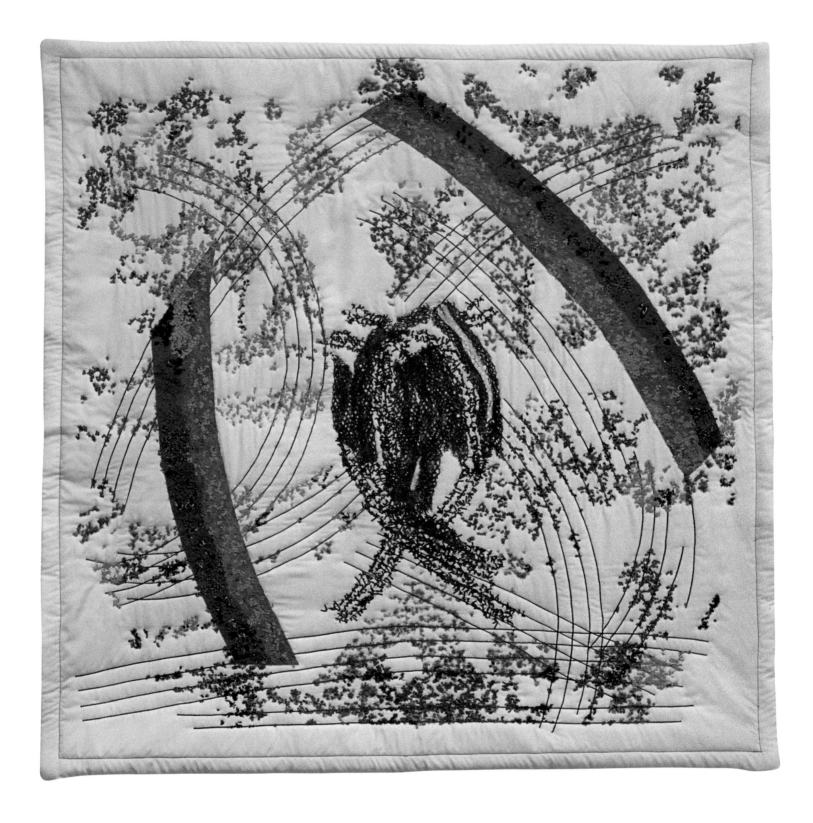

"Love in Chaos" by Marialuisa Sponga, Italy, 2003. This abstract image expresses the artist's inner conflicts. She says, "In the chaos of life within me, I feel the spirit to give a loving and friendly embrace, to convey strength, energy, enthusiasm, solidarity". It is interesting to note that, unlike some artists working in other media, those working in the medium of the quilt, who "paint with fabric", often explain their ideas and inspiration in words.

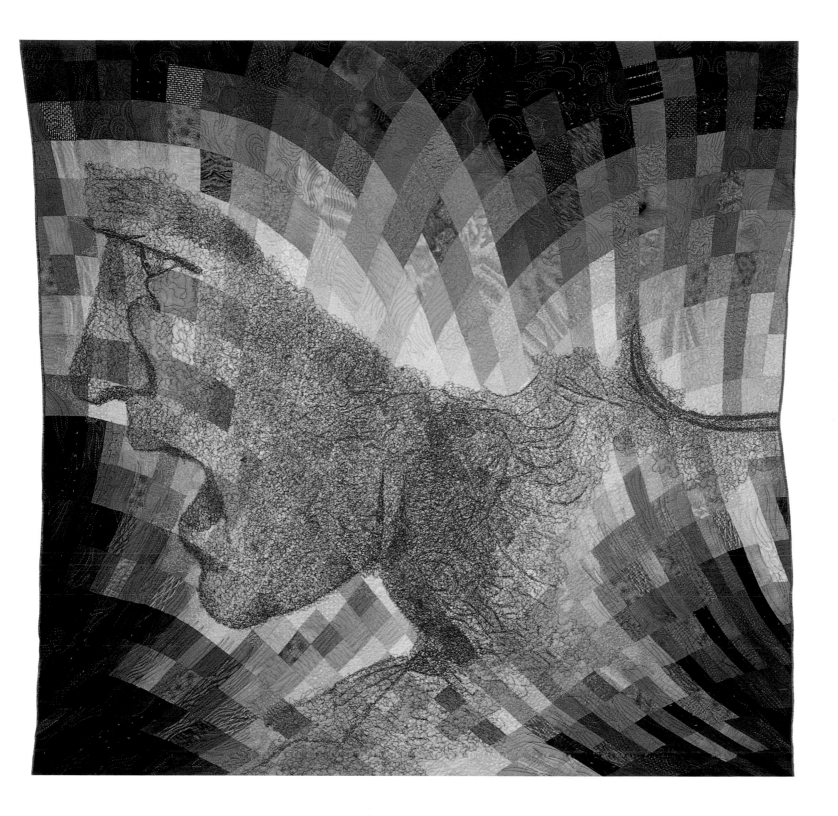

"Le Cri" by Catherine Pascal, Germany, 2001. Inspired by *The Soldier,* a drawing by Leonardo da Vinci that the artist felt expressed her own feelings of depression and anxiety at the time, this also embodies the sense of energy and power that she urgently needed. The background "tiles", she says, symbolize continuity and security, while at the same time giving the visual impression of movement. The background was quilted entirely before the face was embroidered.

"Devoted to my Grandmother: My Bodyguard and Guardian Angel" by Maie Putk, Estonia, 2004. A quilt that embodies both personal and social history, it depicts the artist's first recollection of her grandmother, in the garden in early spring. During her life, Maie's grandmother was her protectress against malicious spirits, and after her death Maie's Guardian Angel. Maie's grandmother's daughters fled from the Soviet regime to America, where they became dressmakers, and the artist acknowledges her debt to her aunts and grandmother, whose love of art and handicraft she has inherited.

"Fossils and Fragments" by Eszter Bornemisza, Hungary, 2004. This quilt is inspired by the historical layers embedded in such things as fossils, and fragments of old city maps that could be read as scripts from the past. The artist's idea is that we can glean meaning from these signs, which will "help us to grasp bits of the mystery of the individual and of history at the same time". A variety of techniques is used to create the complex, textured surface, expressive of the underlying theme of the quilt.

"Souvenir 14, Hellas 2" by Charlotte Yde, Denmark, 2004. A combination of hand-dyed and purchased cottons and scrim, collaged and screen-printed, has been used to create this complex and evocative image, in effect "painting with fabric". The quilt is one of an ongoing series inspired partly by ancient cultures, partly by the artist's own travels.

"Crime Scene #2" by Bente Vold Klausen, Norway, 2004. This quilt is one of a series of works based on photographs of a very well-worn pedestrian walkway in Zurich, the photographs capturing the details of texture and surface used in the design. The white outlined shape on this collage of hand-dyed fabric and textile paint acts both as an important element in the design and as a stimulus to the viewer's imagination: "What has happened here?", we wonder.

"Birthright of Woman" by Ulva Ugerup, Sweden, 2001. This is an exuberant assertion that women should all have the freedom and strength to lay claim to fundamental rights: "...to decide yourself what to wear on your head, to dress as you like, to go dancing, to be an artist, to vote, to walk in peace in your autumn garden, to sing your songs, to read what you like, to be a leopard at heart". These rights are illustrated in a light-hearted way as a series of self-portraits. Quilt artists the world over now follow the time-honoured tradition of using the quilt for conveying messages – personal, political, or religious.

"Dizzy" by Carolyn L. Mazloomi, USA, 2002. Most of this artist's work contains references to African-American life and history. She says: "Quilts connect my body and soul to the music, which has always been an element in my life ... Quilts are my equivalent to making music." She compares the unplanned, improvisational way in which she creates quilts to the rhythms and eloquence of improvised jazz. This is a quilt that pays homage to, and celebrates, the African-American heritage, made as "visual soul food" with the hope that each viewer will "feel the spirit of the cloth".

"Walks in the Woods" by Frieda L. Anderson, USA, 2002. Inspired by walks with her dog, George, in the woods near her home in Elgin, Illinois, this quilt encapsulates the artist's intense appreciation of the whole experience. As well as being a time to reflect on the natural world, the walks are an opportunity to "connect with [her] spiritual world and to visualize where [she wants] to go with her art". George, of course, makes his own, indispensable contribution to a joyful daily event.

"The Edge of the Desert" by Cynthia Morgan, Australia, 2001. This is one of four quilts inspired by a trip in a small aircraft to see Lake Eyre after record-breaking rainfall during the monsoon had filled the normally dry lake. The diverse shapes and colours of the surrounding terrain and the colours of the flooded lake produced by algae and minerals inspired this quilt. It is another example of "painting with fabric" to produce a complex, layered, and textured image reflecting a natural landscape.

BASIC TOOLS AND TECHNIQUES

Many of the quilting traditions described in this book are based on methods and techniques specific to that tradition. To find out more about any of them, please refer to the list of books and resources on pages 217–19. What is given here is a brief outline of some basic methods and techniques that have been known and applied over the years, and which are still used by many contemporary quiltmakers.

TOOLS AND EQUIPMENT

So many aids are available to quiltmakers these days that it would be impossible to list them all. The following are the basic requirements that a beginner will need to use to get started.

For Drafting Patterns and Making Templates (right):

• Cartridge paper and card

• Templates

• Rulers

• Coloured pencils

• Scissors or craft knife

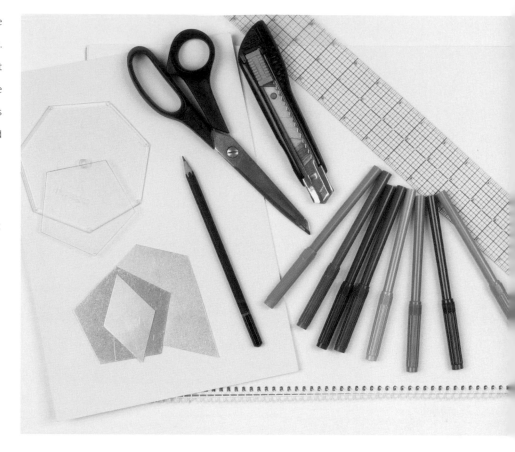

For Sewing (left):

• Cotton patchwork fabrics

• Fabric scissors

• Rotary cutter and self-healing mat (optional, but a very popular way of cutting lots of patches quickly and accurately)

• Needles – various sizes including special quilting needles called "betweens"

• Pins – including long, glass-headed pins

• Threads – all-purpose threads in various colours

• Quilting threads – strong, purpose-made threads in various colours

• Sewing machine (if used)

PATCHWORK

1 Most patterns, especially patchwork blocks, can be drafted on a grid of squares. Draw the pattern full size and identify the shapes needed by outlining them with a fine black marker pen. Use these shapes to make the templates required. Add 6mm (¼in) seam allowance around each shape. You can also use these templates to make appliqué shapes.

2 Draw round the templates onto your chosen fabric, using a soft pencil, and cut out the patch on the line.

3 To stitch by hand, mark in the seam allowance on each patch and sew along it, taking small running stitches. Do not sew into the seam allowance but take a small backstitch before cutting off the thread. If you are using a sewing machine, sew to the end of the line and take one or two backstitches before fastening off.

4 Stitch the block together in units, using 6mm (¼in) seams, then join the units in rows.

5 Join the blocks to make the quilt top. Make the "quilt sandwich" by laying out backing and batting on a large, flat surface. Place the quilt top over them, making sure it has no creases or wrinkles. Use large tacking stitches to anchor the three layers together.

6

7

6 Mark the quilting pattern with a soft pencil, chalk, or special quilt marker.

7 Place the quilt in a frame or hoop and quilt through all three layers.

8 When quilting is complete, finish the edges by trimming the backing and batting evenly with the quilt top and binding them.

9 Pin and stitch the binding to the back of the quilt; or turn the edges of the quilt toward each other and slip-stitch together. Add a label with the maker's name and the date.

9

8

ENGLISH PATCHWORK

1 Buy or make a master template of metal, card, or plastic. Draw around the template on firm paper and cut out as many shapes as you need.

Pin the shapes to fabric and cut around them, leaving a generous seam allowance all the way round.

2 Baste the fabric to the paper, folding the edges over at the corners.

Place the patches right sides together and stitch them by over-sewing the edges.

When the stitching is completed, remove the papers from inside the patches.

1

2

APPLIQUÉ

1 Draw around the templates and cut them out with a seam allowance. Fold over the seam allowance using the drawn line as a guide and baste all the way round. Stitch the shapes to the background using tiny hem stitches.

1

GLOSSARY

ALL-OVER PATTERN A single shape used over the whole quilt surface; also used to describe a quilt top that is pieced from one or more shapes, rather than from blocks (see MOSAIC PATCHWORK, below).

APPLIQUÉ Decorative technique of applying one piece of fabric to the surface of another fabric, either by hand or machine.

BACKING Bottom layer, or lining, of quilt.

BASTING (UK: TACKING) Large running stitches used to anchor work temporarily before final stitching.

BATTING (UK: WADDING) Filling layer placed between the quilt top and the backing.

BLOCK Unit of patchwork, usually a square, that is a complete design in itself. The blocks are sewn together to make a quilt.

BRODERIE DE MARSEILLE Corded and stuffed needlework made in professional Marseilles ateliers during the 17th and 18th centuries.

BRODERIE PERSE Technique involving cutting out printed motifs and applying them to a background fabric.

CABLE TWIST One of many quilting patterns, particularly on wholecloth quilts, that imitate the curves of a rope cable.

COUCHING Embroidery technique in which heavy thread is attached to a background material or design with small stitches.

COURTHOUSE STEPS Version of traditional "Log Cabin" patchwork block in which dark and light strips are placed on opposite sides of the centre square.

CRAZY PATCHWORK Randomly shaped patches in a variety of fabrics are stitched together. The seams are then embellished with embroidery stitches.

DAVID AND GOLIATH Patchwork block pattern based on a 10 x 10 grid of squares, and first published in the 1930s.

DOUBLE WEDDING RING Pieced block design making a pattern of interlocking circles across the surface of the quilt.

DRUNKARD'S PATH Pieced block design in which curved patches are joined to form a pattern of staggered waves. It was possibly named by women of the Temperance Movement, for whom it was a favourite pattern when made in the blue-and-white colours that were emblematic of the Movement.

ENGLISH PATCHWORK Patchwork technique in which the fabric patches are basted over paper templates before being stitched to each other.

FLYING GEESE Patchwork pattern in which right-angled triangles are arranged to resemble the flight-formation of a skein of geese.

FRAME QUILT Style of British patchwork quilt in which a central square is surrounded by a series of borders.

FREE MACHINE-QUILTING Machine-quilting with the machine feed-dogs disengaged.

FREEHAND FEATHERS Traditional feathers quilting pattern marked on the quilt top without the use of templates or stencils.

IKAT Woven fabric in which the pattern is tied and dyed before weaving.

IRISH CHAIN Patchwork block pattern built up from diagonally arranged squares. The name may derive from a weaving pattern of that name.

LOG CABIN Traditional patchwork block in which strips are sewn round a central square, with dark strips on two sides and light strips on the other two.

MARINER'S COMPASS One of many patchwork block patterns in which long triangles radiate from the centre, resembling compass points.

MOSAIC PATCHWORK Technique in which the quilt top is pieced by fitting together geometric shapes, as used in tiled floors and marquetry.

ON POINT The mounting of a square block or patch at an angle so that it appears as a diamond.

ORANGE PEEL Patchwork design using curved patches in the shape of orange segments.

PRESIDENT'S WREATH Early Colonial appliqué block pattern probably named for President Lincoln. Also published as "Rose of Sharon" and "Wreath of Roses".

PRINCESS FEATHER Appliqué block probably derived from the plumes that are emblematic of the Prince of Wales – known as "Prince of Wales Feathers".

ROSE IN A RING Design of roses arranged in a wreath; one of many appliqué block patterns using flowers (of which roses feature most often).

SASHING Strips placed between blocks in a quilt.

SCRIM Durable, loosely woven cotton or linen fabrics, often used for upholstery or as curtain linings.

SEMINOLE Patchwork method developed by the Seminole Indians of Florida, in which narrow strips of fabric are joined, then cut in segments and rejoined to form many patterns.

SHIBORI Collective term in Japanese for a dyeing technique in which fabric is wrapped, folded, or stitched before being immersed in the dye bath. It translates into English as "shaped-resist dyeing".

STAR OF BETHLEHEM Block patchwork pattern in which each of eight points of a star is pieced from diamonds.

STRING PIECING Technique of joining lots of scraps of fabric until they form a piece large enough to cut out patches of the required size and shape for a block.

STRIPPY QUILT Quilt in which the top is made from strips in alternating colours running lengthwise. Quilting patterns are usually worked within the strips.

SUNSHINE AND SHADOW Quilt pattern composed entirely of rows of squares arranged diagonally in alternating colours; particularly popular with Amish quiltmakers. Also known as "Trip Around the World".

TACKING (see BASTING, above)

TIED QUILT Quilt in which the three layers are joined and secured by a series of knots tied at intervals.

TRAPUNTO Technique in which small pieces of batting are inserted from the back of the quilt to give a raised contour to parts of the pattern.

WADDING (see BATTING, above)

WEARDALE CHAIN Quilting pattern of interlinking oval shapes imitating the visual effect of a metal chain. Named after the region in north-east England, where the pattern evolved as part of a strong, regional tradition of wholecloth quilting.

WHIP-STITCH A stitch that holds together two finished edges. The needle is inserted through both fabrics at right-angles to the edges.

WHITEWORK White stitchery used on white fabric. The decorative effect is achieved by contrasts in the shapes and contours of the different stitches and techniques used.

WHOLECLOTH QUILT Quilt top made from a single fabric, sometimes joined to obtain the required size. The quilting may be stitched in decorative patterns or in a simple, utilitarian style.

BIBLIOGRAPHY

GENERAL

GILLOW, John, and Bryan SENTANCE, *World Textiles* (Thames and Hudson, London), 1999

GINSBURG, Madeleine (ed.), *The Illustrated History of Textiles* (Studio Editions, London), 1991

GLASSIE, Henry, *The Spirit of Folk Art* (Harry N. Abraham, Inc. New York), 1989

VON GWINNER, Schnuppe, *The History of the Patchwork Quilt* (Keyser Book Publishing Ltd, Munich; English edition: Schiffer Publishing Ltd, 1988), 1987

HARRIS, Jennifer (ed.), *5000 Years of Textiles* (British Museum Press, London), 1993

RAE, Janet, and Dinah TRAVIS, *Making Connections. Around the World with Log Cabin* (RT Publishing, Chartham, England), 2004

VIBEK DE KONING-STAPLE, Hanne, *Silk Quilts* (The Quilt Digest Press, Chicago), 2000

JAPAN

LANE, Maggie, *Oriental Patchwork* (Charles Scribner's Sons, New York), 1978

LIDDELL, Jill, and Yuko WATANABE, *Japanese Quilts* (Studio Vista, London), 1990

PARKER, Mary, *Sashiko* (Sterling Publishing Co., Inc., New York), 1999

KOREA

DONG-HWA, Huh, and Claire ROBERTS, *Rapt in Colour* (Powerhouse Museum, Sydney and the Museum of Korean Embroidery, Seoul), 1998

INDIA

ASKARI, Nasreen, and Rosemary CRILL, *Colours of the Indus* (Merrell Holberton in association with the Victoria and Albert Museum, London), 1997

GILLOW, John, and Nicholas BARNARD, *Traditional Indian Textiles* (Thames and Hudson, London), 1991

ORMSBY STODDARD, Patricia, *Ralli Quilts* (Schiffer Publishing Ltd, Pennsylvania), 2003

ZAMAN, Niaz, *The Art of Kantha Embroidery* (The University Press Ltd, Bangladesh), 1993

UK

ALLEN, Rosemary, *North Country Quilts and Coverlets* (Beamish North of England Open-Air Museum, Co. Durham), 1987

COLBY, Averil, *Patchwork* (B.T. Batsford Ltd, London), 1958

COLBY, Averil, *Quilting* (B.T. Batsford Ltd, London), 1972

FITZRANDOLPH, Mavis, *Traditional Quilting* (B.T. Batsford Ltd, London), 1954

HAKE, Elizabeth, *English Quilting* (B.T. Batsford Ltd, London), 1937

HULBERT, Anne, *The Complete Crazy Patchwork* (B.T. Batsford Ltd, London), 2002

OSLER, Dorothy, *Traditional British Quilts* (B.T. Batsford Ltd, London), 1987

OSLER, Dorothy, *North Country Quilts* (The Bowes Museum and Friends of the Bowes Museum, Co. Durham), 2001

PARKER, Freda, *Victorian Patchwork* (Anaya Publishers Ltd, London), 1991

RAE, Janet, *The Quilts of the British Isles* (Bellew Publishing Company Ltd, London), 1987

VARIOUS AUTHORS, *Quilt Treasures* (Deirdre McDonald Books in association with the Quilter's Guild of the British Isles, London), 1995

WALES

JONES, Jen, *Welsh Quilts* (Towy Publishing, Carmarthen, Wales), 1997

STEVENS, Christine, *Quilts* (Gomer Press in association with the National Museum of Wales, Ceredigion, Wales), 1993

FRANCE

BERENSON, Kathryn, *Quilts of Provence* (Thames and Hudson, London), 1996

THE NETHERLANDS

MOONEN, An, *Quilts, the Dutch Tradition* (Nederlands Openluchtmuseum, Arnhem), 1992

MOONEN, An, *'T Is al Beddegoet Nederlandse Antieke Quilts, 1650-1996* (uitgave TERRA Zutphen), 1996

SCANDINAVIA

FOSTER, Joan, *Gamle Textiler* (N.W. Damm and Son, Halden, Norway), 2002 (English language version available on CD-Rom)

WETTRE, Åsa, *Old Swedish Quilts* (Interweave Press Inc. Colorado), 1989. (To be re-published by Husqwarna Viking, VSM Group.)

NORTH AMERICA

BACON, Lenice Ingram, *American Patchwork Quilts* (William Morrow and Co. Inc., New York), 1973

BENBERRY, Cuesta, *Always There – The African-American Presence in American Quilts* (The Kentucky Quilt Project, KY), 1992

BETTERTON, Shiela, *Quilts and Coverlets from the American Museum in Britain* (The American Museum in Britain, Bath, England), 1978

BETTERTON, Shiela, *More Quilts and Coverlets from the American Museum in Bath* (The American Museum in Britain, Bath, England), 1991

BEYER, Jinny, *The Quilter's Album of Blocks and Borders* (EPM Publications, Inc., Virginia), 1980

BISHOP, Robert, and Elizabeth SAFANDA, *Amish Quilts* (E.P. Dutton and Co. Inc., New York), 1976

BRACKMAN, Barbara, *Clues in the Calico* (EPM Publications, Inc., Virginia), 1989

BRACKMAN, Barbara, *Encyclopedia of Pieced Quilt Patterns* (Paducah, KY:AQS), 1993

FERRERO, Pat, HEDGES, Elaine, and Julie SILBER, *Hearts and Hands* (The Quilt Digest Press, SA), 1987

FINLEY, Ruth, *Old Patchwork Quilts and the Women Who Made Them*, (Charles T. Branford Co.; first published 1929)

HALL, Carrie A., and Rose G. KRETSINGER, *The Romance of the Patchwork Quilt in America* (The Caxton Printers Ltd, Idaho), 1935

HICKS, Kyra E., *Black Threads* (McFarland and Co. Inc., Jefferson, North Carolina), 2003

HOLSTEIN, Jonathan, *The Pieced Quilt – an American Design Tradition* (New York Graphic Society, Greenwich, Connecticut), 1973

HORTON, Laurel (ed.), *Quiltmaking in America* (Rutledge Hill Press, Inc., Nashville, Tennessee), 1994

JAMES, Michael, *The Quiltmaker's Handbook* (Prentice Hall Inc., Eaglewood Cliffs, NJ; reprinted 1993 Leone Publications, Mountain View, CA), 1978

JENKINS, Susan and Linda SEWARD, *Quilts: The American Story* (Harper Collins, London), 1991

KATZENBERG, Dena S., *Baltimore Album Quilts* (Baltimore Museum of Art, Baltimore), 1981

KHINN, Yvonne, *The Collector's Dictionary of Quilt Names and Patterns* (Acropolis Books Ltd, Washington DC), 1980

LASANSKY, Jeannette (ed.), *Bits and Pieces* (The Oral Traditions Project of the Union County House Historical Society, Lewisburg, PA), 1991

ORLOFSKY, Pat and Myron, *Quilts in America* (McGraw Hill, NY), 1974

WALKER, Marilyn I., *Ontario's Heritage Quilts* (Stoddart Publishing Co. Ltd, Toronto), 1992

WEBSTER, Marie, *Quilts: Their Story and How to Make Them*. Doubleday, Page & Co., NY), 1915

REFERENCES

CENTRAL AMERICA

PULS, Herta, *Textiles of the Kuna Indians of Panama* (Shire Publications Ltd, Bucks., England), 1988

AUSTRALIA

GERO, Annette, *Historic Australian Quilts* (The National Trust of Australia, NSW), 2000

MANNING, Jenny, *Australia's Quilts* (AQD Press, NSW), 1999

ROLFE, Margaret, *Australian Quilt Heritage* (J.B. Fairfax Press Pty Ltd), 1998

NEW ZEALAND

FITZ GERALD, Pamela, *Warm Heritage – Old Patchwork Quilts and Coverlets in New Zealand* (David Bateman Ltd, Auckland, New Zealand), 2003

AFRICA

HARDY, Sandra, *The Tentmakers of Old Cairo* (self-published in England, tel: 01430 423959)

"2003 Masterpieces: Spirit and Strength", Huaqvarna Viking Gallery of Quilt Art, George R. Brown Convention Center, TX, USA. Catalogue of touring exhibition.

ARCHER, Bernice, "The Story of the Changi Quilts", *British Patchwork and Quilting* (Traplet Publications Ltd, Worcs., England), October 2001, pp20–2

BERENSON, Kathryn, "Origins and Traditions of Marseilles Needlework", *Uncoverings: The Journal of the American Quilt Study Group*, 1995, pp7–32

BOYNTON, Linda, "Recent changes in Amish quiltmaking", *Uncoverings: The Journal of the American Quilt Study Group*, 1986, Vol. 6, pp12–46

BRISCOE, Susan, "Focus on Japan", *British Patchwork and Quilting* (Traplet Publications Ltd. Worcs., England), Jan. and Feb. 2004

BROWN, Betha B., "Cuna Molas: The Geometry of Background Fill", *Uncoverings: The Journal of the American Quilt Study Group*, 1982, Vol. 3, pp13–25

COLLINGWOOD, Peter, "Restrained beauty", *Quilters' Review*. Winter, 2002

DAUGHTREE, Sheilah, "Australian Quilting", *British Patchwork and Quilting* (Traplet Publications Ltd, Worcs., England), June 2003, pp16–18

EIKMEIER, Barbara J., "A Style emerges: Korean culture in Contemporary Quilts", *Uncoverings: The Journal of the American Quilt Study Group*, 2001, Vol. 22, pp87–118

FENWICK SMITH, Tina, "Averil Colby: a writer ahead of her time", *Textile Perspectives* (The Quilters' Guild of the British Isles), Summer 2004, pp6–9

HOLLAND, Isobel, "The Old Guard – Canadian Red Cross Quilts", *Popular Patchwork* (Nexus Special Interests, Kent, England), November 2003, Vol. 11, No. 11, pp34–6

JANNIÈRE, Janine, and An MOONEN, *Mosaïques d'Etoffes: A la recherche de l'hexagone*, Musée des Traditions et Arts Normands, Conseil Général de la Seine-Maritime. Exhibition Catalogue, 2003

JANNIÈRE, Janine, "An Important Discovery of French Patchwork", *Antiques Magazine* (New York), Dec. 1995, pp. 822¬9

JANNIÈRE, Janine, "A New World in the Old: European Quilt Scholarship", *The Quilt Journal*, (The Kentucky Quilt Project), 1992, Vol. 1, No. 1, pp4–9

JANNIÈRE, Janine, "Filling In Quilt History: A 16th Century French Patchwork Banner", *The Quilt Journal* (The Kentucky Quilt Project), 1994, Vol. 3, No. 1, pp1–6

JANNIÈRE, Janine, "The Hand Quilting of Marseille", *The Quilt Journal* (The Kentucky Quilt Project), 1993. Vol. 2, No. 1, pp5–9

LONG, Bridget, "A Comparative Study of the 1718 Silk Patchwork Coverlet", *Quilt Studies: The Journal of the British Quilt Study Group* (The Quilters' Guild of the British Isles, Halifax), 2002/3, Issue 4/5, pp54–78

MOONEN, An, "Nederlandse Sitsen Antieke Dekens en Lappendekens in het Nederlands Textielmuseum in Tilburg" ("Dutch chintz antique quilts from private and museum collections in the Textile Museum, Tilburg"), published in Dutch and French in *Quiltmania*, May/June 2003, pp12–17. (www.quiltmania.com)

MOONEN, An, "Quilts in Holland", *Patchwork Tsushin Magazine* (Patchwork Tsushin Co. Ltd, Tokyo, Japan), 2001, Issue 100, pp9–11

OTHER RESOURCES

ON-LINE RESOURCES

An Moonen's Antique Textile website:
www.antiquetextile.info
Information on Dutch quilts.

British Quilt History List: www.quilthistory.co.uk
A forum established primarily for people interested in the history of the British quilt tradition.

International Quilt Study Center, Nebraska:
www.quiltstudy.org

New Pathways into Quilt History:
www.antiquequiltdating.com
Extensive source of information, with articles about the history of quilts in many countries.

Planet Patchwork: www.planetpatchwork.com
Comprehensive patchwork and quilting site

www.quiltethnic.com
Guide to information about the quilting and/or fibre-related art, crafts, and textile traditions of diverse ethnic groups.

Quilt History List: www.quilthistory.com
A forum for people around the world who are interested in antique quilts and related textiles to discuss the historical aspects of quilting.

QuiltStory: www.quilt.co.uk
On-line quilting magazine with features, articles, profiles, UK What's On, and more.

World Wide Quilting Page: www.quilt.com
Comprehensive quilting information

QUILTERS' GUILDS AND NATIONAL ASSOCIATIONS

The American Quilt Study Group
35th & Holdrege East Campus Loop
P.O. Box 4737,
Lincoln, NE 68504-0737 USA
www.h-net.org/~aqsg/

European Quilt Association
www.eqa.ch/

The Quilters' Guild of the British Isles
and The British Quilt Study Group
Room 190, Dean Clough
Halifax, West Yorkshire HX3 5AX
UK
www.quiltersguild.org.uk
(collection of British quilts, by appointment only)

Quilt Study Group of Australia
Dr. Annette Gero
4 Rangers Road
Cremorne
NSW 2090 Australia

QUILT COLLECTIONS

UK

The American Museum in Britain
Claverton Manor
Bath BA2 7BD
Tel: 01225 460503
www.americanmuseum.org

Beamish Open-Air Museum
Beamish
Co. Durham DH9 0RG
Tel: 0191 370 4000
www.beamish.org.uk

Joss Graham – Oriental Textiles
10 Eccleston Street
London SW1W 9LT
Tel: 020 7730 4370
Email: joss.graham@btinternet.com
(quilt collection and shop)

Levens Hall
Kendal
Cumbria LA8 0PD
Tel: 01539 560321
www.levenshall.co.uk

The Manor
Hemingford Grey
Huntingdon
Cambridgeshire PE28 9BN
Tel: 01480 463134
www.greenknowe.co.uk
(Lucy Boston's patchworks: contact Diana Boston)

Museum of Welsh Life
St. Fagans
Cardiff CF5 6XB
Wales
Tel: 029 2057 3500
www.nmgw.ac.uk/mwl

The Quilt Association
Minerva Arts Centre
High Street, Llanidloes
Powys SY18 6BY
Wales
Tel: 01686 413467
www.quilt.org.uk

The Rachel Kay-Shuttleworth Collection
Gawthorpe Hall
Padiham, Burnley
Lancashire BB12 8UA
Tel: 01282 78511
www.rbks.co.uk (CD-Rom available on-line)

Tullie House Museum and Art Gallery
Castle Street, Carlisle
Cumbria CA3 8TP
Tel: 01228 534781
www.tulliehouse.co.uk

Ulster Folk and Transport Museum
Cultra
Holywood
Co. Down
Northern Ireland BT18 0EU
Tel: 02890 428428
www.uftm.org.uk

USA

Museum of the American Quilter's Society
215 Jefferson Street
Paducah, KY 42001-0714
www.quiltmuseum.org

San Jose Museum of Quilts & Textiles
520 South First Street
San Jose, CA 95112-3639
www.sjquiltmuseum.org

MAGAZINES

Australian Patchwork & Quilting
Pride Publishing
PO Box 645
Rozelle
NSW
Australia

Better Homes and Gardens American Patchwork & Quilting
1716 Locust Street
Des Moines, Iowa 50309-3023
USA

British Patchwork and Quilting
Traplet Publications Ltd.
Traplet House, Pendragon Close
Malvern, Worcs WR14 1GA
UK

Fabrications
Grosvenor Exhibitions
High Street, Spalding
Lincs PE11 1YX
UK

Magic Patch
Les Editions de Saxe
20 Rue Croix-Barret 69358
Lyon 07
France

Popular Patchwork
Nexus Special Interests
Nexus House, Boundary Way
Hemel Hempstead
Herts HP2 7ST
UK

Quilter's Newsletter Magazine
741 Corporate Circle, Suite A
Golden, CO 80401
USA

INDEX

ACKNOWLEDGMENTS

I have to thank so many people whose advice and expertise I have called upon in writing this book; it wouldn't have been possible without them. Particular gratitude is due to Janet Rae, Janine Janniere, An Moonen, Laurel Horton, and Tim Longville, all of whom generously gave their time and expertise to check particular areas of my text, and offered comments and advice in its preparation. Any shortcomings, errors, or omissions in the text are entirely my own.

Others who have been immensely helpful are Annette Gero, Joss Graham, John Gillow, Ron Simpson, Tina Fenwick Smith, Sally Ward, Laura Fisher, Herta Puls, Stella Rubin, Kathryn Berenson, Roselind Shaw, Wendy Lugg, Åsa Wettre, Naomi Ichikawa, Helen Joseph, Bridget Long, and Jacqueline Govin.

It has been a pleasure to work both with the Senior Editor, Emily Anderson, and with Emma O'Neil who, as picture researcher, has been indefatigable in tracking down and obtaining the illustrations from sources near and far; their efficiency and co-operation have made my task so much easier. In addition, many people have given invaluable support in sourcing and providing illustrations, including the quilt artists who have given permission for their quilts to be shown. I thank them all and sincerely hope that this book does them the credit they deserve.

Celia Eddy

Mitchell Beazley would like to thank Roger Dixon for his photography and Barbara Mellor and Helen Snaith for their editorial assistance.

Mitchell Beazley would also like to acknowledge and thank the following for their kind permission to reproduce photographs in this book:

Key t top b bottom l left r right OPG Octopus Publishing Group

1 Frieda Oxenham; **2** Sandie Lush; **4** Dr Dianne Firth; **6** Niederrheinisches Museum für Volkskunde und Kulturgeschichte e.V; **7** Museu Nacional de Arte Antiga; José Pessoa; Divisão de Documentação Fotográfica-Instituto Português de Museus; **8** From *Gorgeous Quilts with Japanese Antique Fabric*, Patchwork Tsushin Co, Ltd/Photo Nenji Ayabe; **9** Memling Museum, Druges, Belgium/www.bridgeman.co.uk; **10** © Copyright The Trustees of The British Museum; **11** Photograph courtesy of Joss Graham; **12–13** © The Quilters' Guild of The British Isles; **14** Skinner Inc, Boston & Bolton MA; **15** Stella Rubin Antiques, Darnestown, Maryland/Collection of Eve Gibson/Photo Harriet Wise; **16** From *Patchwork Quilt Tsushin No 118*/Photo Nenji Ayabe/By kind permission of Shizuko Kuroha; **18** Kahotown Educational Committee; **19** Deutsches Textilmuseum, Krefeld; **20** © Photo RMN/© Ravaux; **21** MARUBENI CORPORATION; **22** Photograph courtesy: Kazuo Saito/Private Collection; **23–25** From "Common Threads" exhibition, courtesy of Sue Leighton-White/Photos Wendy Lugg; **26–27** Uesugi Shrine, Yonezawa-city, Yamagata; **28–29** OPG/Roger Dixon/Celia Eddy; **30** From *Patchwork Quilt Tsushin No 118*/Photo Nenji Ayabe/By kind permission of Shizuko Kuroha; **31** From *Gorgeous Quilts with Japanese Antique Fabric*, Patchwork Quilt Tsushin Co, Ltd/Photo Nenji Ayabe; **32–33** From "New International Quilts", exhibition organizer Helen Joseph, Shipley Art Gallery, Tyne & Wear Museums, by kind permission of the artists; **34–37** Huh, Dong-hwa/The Museum of Korean Embroidery; **38** Chunghie Lee; **39** Misik Kim; **40** An Moonen, Antique Textile Specialist and Collector/Nederlands Openluchtmuseum, Arnhem; **41** Christie's Images; **42–45** Photographs courtesy of Joss Graham; **46–47** John Gillow; **48–49** Photographs courtesy of Joss Graham; **50** From "New International Quilts", exhibition organizer Helen Joseph, Shipley Art Gallery, Tyne & Wear Museums/By kind permission of Ranbir Kaur; **51** Lynn Setterington/Photo Steven Yates; **52** V&A Images/Victoria & Albert Museum; **54** Snowshill Costume Collection, Berrington Hall (The National Trust) National Trust Photographic Library/Andreas von Einsiedel; **55** Levens Hall, Cumbria; **56** © The Quilter's Guild of the British Isles; **57** *The Patchworks of Lucy Boston* by Diana Boston/Photo Julia Hedgecoe; **58** © The Quilters' Guild of the British Isles; **59** *The Patchworks of Lucy Boston* by Diana Boston/Photo Julia Hedgecoe; **60–61** Beamish Photographic Archive; **62** Cheltenham Art Gallery & Museums, Gloucestershire, UK/www.bridgeman.co.uk; **63–65** © The Quilters' Guild of the British Isles; **66** © Anne Hulbert/Photo Alan Bennington; **67** © The Quilters' Guild of the British Isles; **68** Photograph © The Bowes Museum/Collection of The Quilters' Guild of The British Isles; **69** Tullie House Museum & Art Gallery; **70** Beamish Photographic Archive; **71** Shipley Art Gallery/Tyne & Wear Museums; **72–75** Beamish Photographic Archive; **76** Sheena Norquay; **77** Helen Parrott – Artist; **78** © *Quilts of The British Isles* by Janet Rae/Deidre McDonald Books 1996/Photo David Cripps; **79** © *Making Connections: Around the World With Log Cabin* by Janet Rae and Dinah Travis/RT Publishing, Chartham, England 2004/Photo Michael Wicks; **80–81** Glasgow City Council (Museums); **82** Pauline Burbidge; **83** Angela Chisholm; **84** From The Jen Jones Welsh Quilt Collection/Roger Clive-Powell; **85–87** From The Jen Jones Welsh Quilt Collection/Peter Davis; **88–89** National Museums and Galleries of Wales; **90** Barbara Howell, Henllan, N Wales; **91** Gwenfai Rees Griffiths; **92–95** The Ulster Folk & Transport Museum MAGNI; **96** Roselind Shaw Quilt, Historian and Collector of Early Irish Patchwork Quilts and Folk Art, N Ireland wjames@hotmail.com; **97** Photo courtesy Grania McElligott/By kind permission of Bryde Glynn; **98** Photo Claude Almodovar © Collection Musée du Vieux-Marseille; **99** Château de Grignan (France); **100** Photos Y Deslandes – Musées Départementaux de la Seine Maritime/"Mosaïques d'étoffes; à la recherche de l'hexagone"/Curator Janine Jannière/Musée des Traditions et Arts Normands/Collection of Janine Jannière, Shelly Zegart, and Jonathan Holstein; **101** Christie's Images; **102** Photo Claude Almodovar © Collection Musée du Vieux-Marseille; **103 t** Musée des Tissus/Pierre Verrier; **103 b** Museon Arlaten, musée départemental d'ethnographie, Arles; **104** Photo Claude Almodovar © Collection Musée du Vieux-Marseille; **105** Photo Y Deslandes – Musées Départementaux de la Seine Maritime/"Mosaïques d'étoffes; à la recherche de l'hexagone"/Curator Janine Jannière/Musée des Traditions et Arts Normands/Famille Garandeau; **106–107** Kathryn Berenson; **108** Musée des Tissus/Pierre Verrier; **109** Photo Claude Almodovar © Collection Musée du Vieux-Marseille; **110** Studio Ethel/Musée de la Toile de Jouy, Jouy-en-Josas; **111** Geneviève Attinger; **112** Quilt & photo An Moonen Collection; **113** An Moonen, Antique Textile Specialist and Collector/Nederlands Openluchtmuseum, Arnhem; **114** An Moonen, Antique Textile Specialist and Collector/ Zuiderzeemuseum, Enkhuizen; **115–116** An Moonen, Antique Textile Specialist and Collector/Nederlands Openluchtmuseum, Arnhem; **116–117** An Moonen, Antique Textile Specialist and Collector/Simon van Gijn Museum, Dordrecht; **118** An Moonen, Antique Textile Specialist and Collector/Akka Philips, Middelie; **119** Dirkje van der Horst-Beetsma/Photo Diana Post; **120–121** From *Old Swedish Quilts* by Åsa Wettre/Photos Lena Nessle/Private Collection; **122** From *Old Swedish Quilts* by Åsa Wettre/Photo Lena Nessle/Jönköpings läns museum; **123** From *Old Swedish Quilts* by Åsa Wettre/Photo Lena Nessle/Åsa Wettre Collection; **124–125** From *Old Swedish Quilts* by Åsa Wettre/Photos Lena

Nessle/Jönköpings läns museum; **126** Maija Brummer/www.kolumbus.fi/maija.brummer; **127** Katriina Flensburg quiltakademin@swipnet.se; **128** Ron Simpson; **130** Courtesy of The Peabody Essex Museum; **131** Accession number M972.B.1 McCord Museum of Canadian History, Montreal; **132** Stella Rubin Antiques, Darnestown, Maryland; **133** © Museum of Fine Arts, Houston, Texas, USA, The Bayou Bend Collection, gift of Miss Ima Hogg/www.bridgeman.co.uk; **134** Stella Rubin Antiques, Darnestown, Maryland/Photo Harriet Wise; **135** Stella Rubin Antiques, Darnestown, Maryland; **136–137 t** LAURA FISHER/Antique Quilts and Americana, New York City; **137 b** Stella Rubin Antiques, Darnestown, Maryland; **138** Janet Steadman/Photo Roger Schreiber; **139** Elizabeth Cave/From the collection of the University of Nebraska; **140** Christie's Images; **141–142** LAURA FISHER/Antique Quilts and Americana, New York City; **143** Stella Rubin Antiques, Darnestown, Maryland; **144–145** Courtesy John & Arlene Volk/Amish Country Lanes/www.amishcountrylanes.com; **146** Stella Rubin Antiques, Darnestown, Maryland/Photo Harriet Wise; **147** LAURA FISHER/Antique Quilts and Americana, New York City; **148** Stella Rubin Antiques; Darnestown, Maryland; **149–150** Christie's Images; **151** LAURA FISHER/Antique Quilts and Americana, New York City; **152** Skinner Inc, Boston and Bolton MA; **153** LAURA FISHER/Antique Quilts and Americana, New York City; **154** Skinner Inc, Boston and Bolton MA; **155** Christie's Images; **156** Judy Severson; **157** "Jacobean Arbor" by Patricia B. Campbell, Dallas, Texas, www.patcampbell.com; **158** © Museum of Fine Arts, Boston, Massachusetts, USA, Bequest of Maxim Karolik/www.bridgeman.co.uk; **159** LAURA FISHER/Antique Quilts and Americana, New York City; **160** Old State House Museum, 300 West Markham St, Little Rock, Ar USA; **161** LAURA FISHER/Antique Quilts and Americana, New York City; **162** LAURA FISHER/ Antique Quilts and Americana, New York City; **163** Stella Rubin Antiques, Darnestown, Maryland; **164** LAURA FISHER/Antique Quilts and Americana, New York City; **165** Lisa Louise Adams/Photo Macario; **166** OPG/Roger Dixon/Sally Ward; **167** OPG/Roger Dixon/Jo Matkin; **168–171** Herta Puls, Textile Artist, Designer, Collector of Indigenous Textiles; **172** Charlotte Patera/www.charlottepatera.com; **173** Christel Walter/Photo Ulrich Reiß; **174–176** National Gallery of Australia, Canberra; **177** Permission has been granted to reproduce this photograph of the Elizabeth Keen quilt by the Queenscliffe Historical Museum (Victoria, Australia). It is a significant item in the textiles collection at the Museum; **178** National Gallery of Australia, Canberra; **179** Courtesy: Powerhouse Museum, Sydney, Australia; **180** Gay Epstein; **181** National Wool Museum, Geelong; **182** Australian War Memorial Museum, Negative Number 14235; **183** Australian War Memorial Museum, Negative Number 32526; **184–185** Photograph courtesy of *New Zealand Quilter* magazine, www.nzquilter.com; **186** B.024725 Museum of New Zealand Te papa Tongarewa; **187** B.028823 Museum of New Zealand Te Papa Tongarewa; **188** Courtesy Wendy Lugg; **189** Marge Hurst/ Photo Julia Brooke-White; **190** Copyright: Museum of Cultural History, University of Oslo, Norway/Photographer Ingvild Sonstad; **192** John Gillow; **193** Photograph courtesy of Joss Graham; **194** From "New International Quilts", exhibition organizer Helen Joseph, Shipley Art Gallery, Tyne & Wear Museums, permission of Sandra Hardy and Tarok Fattoh, Sandra Hardy Gallery, South Cave; **195** From "New International Quilts", exhibition organizer Helen Joseph, Shipley Art Gallery, Tyne & Wear Museums, by kind permission of Sally Scott; **197** Dorothy Stapleton; **198** C June Barnes; **199** From "New International Quilts", exhibition organizer Helen Joseph, Shipley Art Gallery, Tyne & Wear Museums, by kind permission of Effie Galletly; **200** Ann Fahy/The Ulster Folk and Transport Museum MAGNI; **201** Ted Storm-van Weeldon, Netherlands/Gerard van Yperen; **202** Marialuisa Sponga-Italy-www.sponga.com; **203** Catherine Pascal; **204** Maie Putk from Estonia; **205** Eszter Bornemisza; **206** Charlotte Yde/www.yde.dk; **207** Bente Vold Klausen; **208** Ulva Ugerup, textile artist, Sweden, ulvaugerup@hotmail.com; **209** Carolyn L. Mazloomi; **210** Quilt artist Frieda Anderson, Elgin, Illinois, USA; **211** Cynthia Morgan, Caloundra, Australia, cynthiamorgan@cynthiamorgandyequilts.com; **212–215** OPG/Roger Dixon/C. Eddy.